# Plea of the Valueless

**Proposing Economic Equality**

BY
PAUL PROGEN

Published by
Paul Progen
Yi'ima Printing, Inc.
2385 John Fries Highway
Quakertown, PA 18951
views@28thForum.org
CitizensValue.org

# DEDICATION

This book is dedicated to all future generations. May the hardships they endure on the path to economic equality bear the fruit of peace and prosperity!

# TABLE OF CONTENTS

# PREFACE

I am driven to write by anger, frustration, and exhaustion, and I do so within a democracy influenced by the pressures of materialism. I live in a cocoon where I am unable to buy influence, even the smallest portion that would represent my living presence in this democracy. I have scoured this political wrapping in search of a way out, a way to be equal to those who buy influence but to no avail, with the exception that my imagination has grasped a way to win through this struggle. I'm disappointed to realize that the influence bought by power and wealth holds persuasion to the turns I decide to take on as I make my way through life. Having examined the course of my life and worked with great diligence toward understanding these disappointments, I am angry to see that the twisted yarn of politics is interfering with living life in accordance with the ideals laid out in the Constitution and that I have no influence toward making the changes that need to occur. I am frustrated that I should expect my progeny to spend their life in the same way, constitutionally valueless and without a right to influence. I am exhausted from empathizing with a lifetime of complaints that will only be answered at the discretion of the influential.

I have written this book so that others may envision a

path to economic equality. I have acknowledged that influence has directed the course of government and law, and that common people have had little to do when deciding that course. Common sense can prove that all people continue to advance societies and create wealth that continues to be guaranteed by our collected potential. Visualizing a way in which common people can be recognized for the potential they bring and the influence they should have—but do not, I am obligated by necessity to point the way economic equality can be written into our Constitution and guarantee an equality of influence.

I am inspired by the beauty and magnificence of my grandchildren, that they should have a better life than me. This phrase alone, which all of humanity claims for itself and we all claim individually, serves to anoint a positive potential in all humanity.

Humbled and brought to tears with the knowledge that the innocence my grandchildren possess will lessen with every day that passes, I have lived to recognize that ideals still remain after innocence is corrupted by reality, and I will do everything I possibly can so that they may have better ideals to hold onto than did I.

Every person should have the right to an equal measure of influence. To have that influence, every person needs to have an equal measure of value. We can ascertain our value and use it as influence to easily and constructively participate in our government and benefit our society. The guarantee of influential participation of average citizens will hasten the rise of economic equality. I am not constitutionally recognized as having value. In the eyes of my government, a penny is more valuable than I am. It has one-cent worth of influence. I want my grandchildren and the next generations to have what I do not: value!

# 1.

## *ORIGIN AND CONCEPT*

# 1.1.

## *Influence*

THE SUBJECT OF INFLUENCE IS a central focus to finding economic equality. Economics and equality are separated by a great divide and influence is the wedge deciding the expanse of that disparity regardless that influence and matters of finance are intertwined. For the good of optimism and harmony, we will start by understanding the presence of economic inequality as a result of past occurrences. The achievement of economic equality rests with understanding equality to be an application as opposed to being a result. Equality is something to be used and applied in the same way influence and finance are put to use. We must decide our morality, fortitude and obligation to construct a method of braiding influence, economics and equality into one strong and enduring rope. To be concise and explain with brevity the peculiarities of influence is my first endeavor. Going further to explore a concept of equality whose fabric is woven from influence, politics, and economics is the foundation of this entire undertaking.

Possession of influence assures inequality in its favor. We are imposed upon by influence whether we like it or not, and its possession dictates the degree of that imposition. When we acquire the capital to control influence, imposition occurs to a lesser degree than when we have no means. Possession and imposition are at contest for balance, like a seesaw: the closer they are positioned to the fulcrum, the smoother the ride. Possession of control and the imposition of control it can dictate is the reward of influence. Cunning use of influence can leverage everything from advancement to destruction while the skill and manipulation of its practice is an art to be mastered. Its toolbox is brimming with everything from encouragement to intimidation. Our society is accustomed to impositions of all sorts, and defending them from the exercise that possession of influence initiates and controls is routine. The survival of those imposed by influence has no choice but to be avoided, which is not all together possible. In modern times, the possession of influence is decided by its financial status, which in turn decides economic inequality at the discretion of those with possession. To be deprived of some possession of influence means being deprived of economic equality. The experience of economic equality relies upon the equal exercise of finance to ascertain a possession of influence.

Possession and imposition are two distinct and opposing aspects of influence. In the contest between the two, possession is nimble and often appears well positioned to have the upper hand. Imposition relies upon endurance to continue the fight. Seldom does imposition become possession, but when it does its impact is unmistakable.

4

How deep possession wants to cut into, encumber, or incapacitate imposition is a measure of its shrewdness. Implementation, execution, and restraint to use influence are personal responsibilities of possession. When possession unleashes these responsibilities, imposition feels their intensities as they occur. We don't know precisely to what degree influences will injure imposition so deeply to cause disruptions and retaliations. We only know of its possibilities and probabilities.

Those with the wherewithal are presented with the opportunity to practice influence. Possession, affordability, and the exercise thereof work cohesively to control influence. One may inquire to the necessary appreciation needed to apply influence. When those subjected to influence realize affordability and possession are hand in hand, the appreciation needed to implement its use makes no difference. They only know the influence placed upon them is paid for by some other entity. The prosperity needed to obtain influence only matters to those managing the expense of its price. The only reason to afford the cost of influence is in the acquisition of its control. The imbalance of control on decisions that affect everyone distinguishes an inequality founded through money and resources. This sounds like the definition of economic inequality.

The illusiveness of influence becomes a part of everyday life and ingrained to the point where we are both conscious and unconscious to that which sways our reactions. We can't always define or don't take the time to examine every count of influence placed upon us. The components of influence—possession, imposition, control, and impact—mingle together with material and abstract applications and yield an outcome that is immeasurable. The consequence of influence reverberates in all directions and in so many ways. As we come closer to examining influence and its depths, its aspects increase. When we picture the complexities of influence we perceive infinity of pixels. Who is the genius that can answer the possible number of outcomes that resulted from influence? The possibilities and results derived from influence in all its forms are infinite.

Coincidental to our evolution, we have cultivated different associations to influence. The influences we initiate have advanced as we have progressed, and their economic ties have developed alongside. Prior to making influence equally available, we must decipher the type of influence that should be employed. To identify that which is appropriate, we need to understand and separate different influences by their features. We will choose to permit application of influence whose virtue assures equality. Upon assessment of those virtues, we shall seek influence, the use of which will abate inequitable influences presently imposed upon all.

\* \* \*

FROM THE BEGINNING, INFLUENCE WAS established by mankind's natural and instinctive use of raw brutal power to achieve domination. It is no stretch of the imagination to point out that the use of physical brutality has been instrumental in gaining what one wants. Whether that use of brute power is achieved through the assertion of one individual or through a combination of individuals, its imposition upon another always influences a decided response. Relative to different perspectives or circumstances involved, those consequential responses may be wanted or unwanted, popular or unpopular. For instance, the desire to preserve one's life and, at the same time, to disavow one's personal commitment or ethics, however temporary or masked, is in total a response influenced by the power imposed upon it. Alternatively, the wanted decision to assert brutality upon another imposes influence resulting in innumerable decided and unpredictable responses. In the same cycle of imposition and response, raw power and the threat of its use continues to be influential in the negotiation of peace or war. The necessity for preserving individual and communal survival rests with the ability to negotiate against the use of raw brutal power. We have seen instances where congruous application of ethics and knowledge has strengthened negotiation and diminished the ability of domination by means of raw power.

Progress will mitigate brutal influence in the world only with the continued insertion and influence of knowledge and the growth of intelligence. If an aggressively violent individual or group is to be quelled and, consequently, for influence to be taken away from them, it will be done only with the use of greater intelligence combined with the discretion of asserting a counter form of brutal influence. Intelligence continues to have a greater effect in determining influence. Intelligence enables mass civility to occur and offers the opportunity and ability to increase its influence, thus diminishing influence determined by physical means.

Creative utilizations of intelligence have fostered and ushered in the use of material influence, which has been more commonly sanctioned to offset brutal influence. Today, material influence, money, goods, and supplies are used as an incentive or discipline to sway decisions made by individuals, groups, or nations. It is important to recognize the difference between brutal influence and material influence because of the expansive nature of material influence. The perceived values and incomprehensible applications of material influence are seemingly infinite in their own claim. From money to valuables to services and the promises thereof, and the multitude of possible reciprocations and their outcomes, the use of material influence carries a different value in each instance. While brutal influence utilizes direct and indirect manners of physical force, material influence relies upon means to avoid physical force. Now, if nonphysical influences were to be applied, they would require greater knowledge, deliberation, and resources.

I will continue to use the phrase "material influence" as a description of influence imposed or gained by the use, and/or promise, of money, or objects, services, and favors that can be translated to having a monetary value, regardless of the debate of that value.

For the most part, any valuable consideration given or promised with an expected outcome to compromise the receiver's behavior, whether it is used to serve a good or bad purpose, concerns the concept of material influence. Bribery is a matter of material influence in that it seeks to compromise integrity. In the case of a bribe, the profit gained from the barter of material influence is generally contained by the parties involved, while all others lose with no prospect of recovery. Charity is a matter of material influence that seeks to compromise loyalty. If material influence is offered as a charity, it is hoped to gain loyalty with the expectation of manifesting profitably for at least one party, if not both. A financial agreement is a matter of material influence that openly displays a particular compromise from both parties with an often predictable outcome. A promise can be a matter of material influence when that promise seeks to elicit profitability for one party or both. While material influence does not necessarily require a response, it is often assumed that it will manifest one regardless of how tangible the response is. Gifts and donations are subtle forms of material influence that may be accompanied by an undercurrent of expectation to which its fulfillment is understood to be relaxed. The outcome from the use of material influence is generally never guaranteed. Even in the case of financial agreements, the outcome is often disputed and left for outside institutions to resolve.

One aspect of survival is that we are consistently nudged, pushed, and pulled with influences throughout our lives from beginning to end. Thankfully, civilization has advanced from a time when influence was asserted with brutal force to our present age when material influence is used with greater frequency. This means, as a civilized society, we should be able to live our lives without the threat or imposition of physical harm. We are expected, however; to substitute the barter of material influence as relief to the impositions of brutal influence. We take responsibility to find our own zones of living comfortably and cooperatively with those we become connected through this bartering. The give and take of material values is common in our daily interactions and we have become proficient in knowing the profits we wish to gain in those interactions. Having acquired some understanding and experience in the dealings of a world stressed with material influence, we have found the need to digest a different influence prevalent to our day: a need driven by the influence of information filled with truths and lies, accuracies, and inaccuracies.

An objective in the use of influence is to ascertain both material- and thought-evoked values. The monetization of information originates by initiating material influence and results in both distinguishable and undistinguishable values. Monetary value derived from the presentation of information such as commercials is distinguishable. Monetary value derived from opinions and commentaries is not specifically distinguishable except to the intentions of the creator. Nonetheless, our skill to distinguish value consequential of influence delivered through information is measured differently than discovering value consequential of influence delivered through material transmission.

I describe infusions of power to gain influence using

these three terms: brutal influence, material influence, and information influence. Our inability to classify, differentiate, and describe strict borders allows influence to seep outside its obvious adherence. This becomes most apparent when we inspect details of the effects of influence after its implementation. Each case of influence imposed can result in combinations to which I have used terms describing their input and outcomes, however specifically imprecise those descriptions may be to the instance. The business model of organized crime uses combinations of brutal and material influences while restricting the release of information. Super PACs expense funds toward material influences such as campaign financing, and information influences such as opinionated and commentary advertising. Facebook's use of information and its dissemination has caused us to examine the profit of information influence from perspectives of both monetized and thought provoked gains.

In order to adjust our loyalties and maintain our integrity, we must decipher all of the influences placed upon us, and this includes influences that are introduced to us from within ourselves as opposed to influences that stem from "outside" sources. Or to put this another way, the distinction here is to understand the difference between our own development of an idea that we've considered from that of an idea that has been introduced to us, something that we suddenly learn that has the potential to alter a previously held view. We have quickly come to a point where disparate information plays a much larger role in how its persuasions permeate us, which is to say that information was never as readily available and widespread as it is today and will be in the future. This challenges us to decipher a bombardment of information and to then compartmentalize that information appropriately, to separate the wheat from the chaff. It is not surprising that myriad information has become a more relevant manner utilized to compromise our loyalties. The profitability of information is a defining characteristic and is frequently left opaquely undefined. Who is intended to gain the most is often the main question. The answer relies upon the motives of the giver in the information that is transferred. I will continue to use the phrase "information influence" as a description of influence imposed or gained by the use of information regardless of that information's intention and integrity or whether it is sought or is an obvious or subliminal intrusion.

A free offering of valid information, as in the sharing of knowledge and established facts, profits the recipient in the least and it is only upon one's perception of that information where its constructiveness is determined. If shared knowledge is used for destructive means, then it may only be the recipient and giver that perceive a constructive nature in the sharing of such knowledge. While it is hoped that knowledge sharing is always constructive, it must be assumed that this is not always the case. From a different perspective, a free offering of distorted, manipulated, and even fictional information that seek to compromise our emotions is, at the very least, intended to profit the giver. Preying upon guilt, patriotism, empathy, sympathy and so many more emotions is a crafty plea of information influence. It is entirely upon the recipient's dissemination, interpretation and reconstruction as to how that influence can or will be used. With the offering of information, only the giver fully understands what they expect to gain. All others that look to examine the information's intention can only assume who will profit and what may be gained or lost.

In the past, the many ways in which information was delivered were limited and often monitored. Today, with the advent of open communication resources including the World Wide Web and social media, information is abundant. Information can be used to infiltrate all aspects of life: personal, social, and professional. The scope of this infiltration is not monitored well and allows for unresolved questions of censorship. Censorship and its applications are disorganized as a result of the intentions and opinions of the varying parties that make up our global community. Each nation, relative to the manner in which they govern, has contributed a different opinion in regard to the presentation of information and the influence this information may have. Every nation has expressed or allowed the expression of information influence by its own government and their citizens regardless of their efforts toward censorship or suppression. In regard to total suppression of that influence, a nation's expression is made in that saying nothing is saying something. The concept of free speech has allowed for open debate and is an expressive form of information influence; by contrast, propaganda is a calculated and organized form of information influence. However varying in their goals, all of these forms of information influence simply provide or suppress information, or express a variety of suppositions, for the recipient to interpret.

Our modern means of access and the ability for the majority population of the world to seek and gather information makes todays societies the most well informed to date. However, in no way does this imply that groups of people, sections of society or nations act intelligently as a whole. It does mean to say that individuals are capable of asserting intelligence given their access to information and growth of personal knowledge. The common dilemma becomes how the assertion of individual opinion is diminished when groups of people mass together to resolve a problem. Presently, we complain, protest, and voice opinions that we expect to be properly addressed in government. Alas, many problems continue and at times go entirely unrecognized at the whim of whatever governing party. This dilemma has a simple solution: to allow the individual citizen a means of material influence as an expression and representation of each citizen's concerns. In every case and for every concern however great or small, however long or short term, an amassing of the citizen's material influence will provide society with majority opinions and counter opinions, which can be organized and used constructively toward resolving any and all issues.

One can presume, upon writing the Constitution and the Bill of Rights, the founders made an attempt to connect material influence to the presumption of intelligence in a certain segment of citizens. This attempted connection was poorly conceived because the right to vote was granted only to those who owned land. The attachment between a citizen's material wealth and the necessary intelligence to gain such wealth may be judged as the founder's precursor between influence and intelligence. Perhaps the founders believed that illiterate and poorly educated citizens should not have any influence in dictating their opinions and concerns to their representation. This presumption plays to a difference between the time of the Constitution's writing and today when not only our nation's population but the world population is largely literate and maintains immediate unlimited access to information and a greater pool of knowledge. Now, to fast forward to the present day, while every citizen's right to influence—that is, to vote— was eventually gained, any material right to influence has been lost. The ownership of land, as a principle material right to influence, has been appropriately removed, but no material right to influence, recognizing all citizens equally, has replaced what has been removed. The difference between vocally influenced representation and materially influenced representation goes unrecognized.

Our vote is a vocal expression of influence. The result is the same when a vote is counted, whether it is a voiced exclamation in a boardroom or the halls of congress or stuffing a ballot box or pressing a touch screen. A material expression of influence is much more than vocal. It requires the application of value to express influence.

The operation of every government to have ever

existed has been affected by random insertions of material influence and yet none have ever guaranteed its citizens the counteraction of the same type of influence. This, in itself, leaves the concept of democracy unfulfilled. Conjecture or not, with or without intention, our founders may have been onto something that they did not recognize or could not formulate and express properly: a deliberate connection between a citizen's material influence and their representation in government. Such an influence that represents the citizen is intended to balance random influences and sway the decision process in government. This inability to possess and use a material influence has resulted in an obstructed connection between the citizen population and their representatives. It is perhaps only now, due to a greater base of knowledge and continued access of information among the citizen population, that material influence will have the possibility of being asserted through an amendment to the United States Constitution. That material influence amounts to having the ability to put one's money where one's mouth is.

Presently, the right to vote does not address the concerns of the citizen population. Regardless of the origin and volume of material influence used toward propping up potential representatives, American citizens are still responsible for asserting their vocal wealth: voting a representative into office. The present-day dilemma of the loyalty a representative should have automatically places that representative in a precarious position. On one hand, it is the citizen's vote and their representation that should demand the greatest loyalty. On the other hand, such loyalty to the citizen has become diluted by the material influence that has propped a representative into the position of their success and continues to nudge them during their tenure. That an established and permitted material influence dictates any degree of loyalty from representation while any hint of disregard to equitably represent every citizen exists when no such influence can be dictated from the citizens themselves, is a form of corruption and requires change. In order to help the citizen's representatives balance their loyalties appropriately, the populace needs a direct link to convey their influence that stems from crediting them their material value. Ultimately, it is important that the citizen population is not overshadowed in any way, by any other influence, in connection to their political representation.

Given the decision process that a political representative must go through and the concerns they must consider toward all the assets that make up our present-day society, the influences nudging our democracy need not be taken down. It is important to recognize that business, industry, and wealth have a great deal to do with the ongoing success of our nation. It is through the concept of capitalism that innovation, drive, and determination to succeed is found. It is through business and industry that sustenance is attained for the populace. There is nothing abnormal in the effort and resolve of wealth and power to seek influence in governing a mass of people. The common citizen should look upon that particular level of tenacity as an asset rooted in some aspects of governance that serve in their interest as well. That same citizen should also seek to counterbalance the influence asserted in the political system so that their concerns and access to representation is not overshadowed.

Our political system lacks a citizen's material influence, which result is in an imbalance of overall influence in representation. For any democracy to continue a protracted existence, it is necessary to balance all the aspects that create its function. When the concerns of this citizen population are compromised by other influences, the resulting decision process cannot be in the interests of all assets, assuming the nation's citizens are considered an asset at all. The citizens of the United States contribute in innumerable ways beyond taxation. Through these contributions, the citizens are of value. It is confounding that the American citizen is valueless in the sense of material influence toward their representation when value given by nominal entities is permitted and the decision to permit either of these rests in the legal entitlement of the citizen's representatives. It is no wonder that the citizens look upon their representatives with dismay, extracting value from them while providing opaque benefit. It is doubly insulting when those same representatives permit themselves excuses for their dysfunctionality to execute governmental responsibilities. Adding injury to insult, the citizens of this nation perceive that their concerns are being placed in the background while the often well-funded and isolated interests of their representatives are placed in the foreground. It is unacceptable that representation has used many differing opacities permitting them to maintain excuses in the guiding of their loyalties. It is time for our representation to be firmly guided by the citizen population through a legal and equitable expression of material influence.

From a different perspective, apart from of the present-day protections of the United States Constitution, it can be said that there is little difference between our government as a democracy and any other type of governing. If a greater influence, as founded individually or through corporate wealth, overshadows the voice and influence of all the citizens, then one can determine that the type of governing that is being instituted is anything other than a complete democracy. In a desire to come closer to completing our democracy, it will be necessary for the citizens to have influence, asserted through their representation, as great as or greater than any other influence. At this time, this does not exist in the United States. The material influence applied toward representation overwhelmingly resides in corporate America and wealthy individuals. In the perspective of different types of governing, whether it is our democracy, a monarchy, an autocracy or a communist regime, the decision process resides in very few influential individuals. If it is true that corporate America and wealthy individuals have greater influence in our political decision process, then it is accurate to say that our Constitution has not yet fulfilled the concepts that complete, or come closer to completing a true democracy. Asserting material influence as a constitutional right of the citizen is the only measure that can be taken at this time that will definitively identify the truest form of democracy available to mankind, at this point in our economic and political evolution.

# 1.2.

## *Time and space*

EACH ENTITY IN EXISTENCE IS given an unspecified time to exist. For now, planet Earth is the space we are given to use that time. As humans, we have evolved many collective influences such that our interconnected technological abilities have reached a point in which coexistence is necessary and unavoidable. As we continue to advance in this manner, avoiding self-annihilation will require uniform recognition and respect for the contributions of all the peoples of the world. Coexistence is necessary. We need to learn how to live together, and if we don't, the prospect of annihilating ourselves could become real. The system we currently have in place leads us to believe that annihilation is more probable than coexistence. The idea of relieving brutal influence, equating material influence and properly utilizing information influence to foster a new direction in our evolution is paramount to our global existence.

Although I point out the need to correct the United States Constitution to include material recognition of its citizen's contributions, an understanding of material influence should be applied worldwide. Along with an opportunity to continue American worldwide leadership, the United States can also spearhead a global effort to ultimately remove brutal and material influences as obstacles, and begin to understand suitable implementations of information influence. This will be no easy task. Each nation will have to approach its governmental policies and meld a restructuring to include its citizen's material influence. I perceive this to be an easier task within a democratized structure and suggest that the United States Constitution is easily capable of including an amendment that recognizes its citizen's material influence. It would be an amendment that would broaden the scope of equality, fulfill the concept of democracy, and honor the existing constitutional structure without interference. With the absorption of this proposal we would have a capable concept whose purpose and means would serve to conquer the issue of material influence, a concept that would extend worldwide and move us forward together and contribute toward a global filtering of information influence and thereby lead to a productive understanding of its use. This, for sure, will foster a new direction in our evolution of influential applications used in our global existence.

Let's remember that the literal space we take up involves a measure of material influence that is different than taxation and its uses. Worldwide taxation processes build societies and at the same time permit disassociations between governments, the tax users, and their influentially deprived taxpayers. In return for my effort and contribution, I expect to be influential toward negotiating solutions that pertain to common concerns. The only way that I can emphasize my opinion is to make my money instrumental to the concern that I wish to become involved. I expect to have a constitutional right recognizing my value and influence. I wish it were different, but "if you can't beat them, you'll have to join them." Throughout the course of time societies have grown to resolve issues by leaning upon the voice of the influential few. Past and present influence, and the way it has affected government, has never been nor will ever be, removed from human aspiration. So why should I be left out, a contributor unrecognized for my value. I want my influential voice to be leaned upon. I want to get past the issue of being realized for my material influence and grow into understanding our information-influenced future. I recognize and acknowledge the scope and purity of removing all material influence from the function of government. How magnificent the concept and how incapable our abilities are, to completely remove all material influences! I would be incredibly naïve to think that any evolved social habit, such as applying influence, could be changed or removed. So I come to a pragmatic conclusion: I demand my measure of influence as a constitutionally protected right. Until I get it and all the peoples of the world get it, there will never be a resolution toward gaining equality. Fragmentation throughout different societies and in many different ways will continue to occur.

Because we are social individuals living in an interconnected environment we are encouraged to interact responsibly toward each other with mutual respect and influence. However, our present patterns of social fragmentation permit the narrowing of our individual responsibilities toward coexistence. We need to enable an individual desire, a reason to want to participate in a mutually respectful coexistence. We have coalesced into recognizable groups we perceive to be compassionate toward our political concern. However, those groups have distorted influences and created unbalanced opaque representations toward resolving mutual concerns. Worldwide, granting an application of equitable influence can diminish the individual scale of social disrespect. It is through our right of equitable influence, here in the United States, through our Constitution, that we can increase a desire toward mutual recognition and respect and consequently demonstrate its function to the world. In essence, we seek to exercise our individual influential responsibility as a prevention and deterrent from continuing social erosion and fragmentation. We want to be respected individually. We require an avenue that permits us to respect others socially. We want that avenue to have a transparent balanced representation and a means to contribute our social responsibility. If we are to have this avenue, we must construct it. Currently, it is not locatable on any available map.

It is an understanding of my complaint—that I vote but have no equitable influence—that has caused me to dissect and articulate a solution. Doing so provides for a greater voice than I can possibly present by taking to the streets and shouting my woes. It is for my purpose and a greater purpose—for those who have taken to the streets in earnest representation of their concerns—that I articulate my complaint and go further to discuss and offer a solution. That solution, in its broad context, will allow for those who have expressed their concerns through present social discourse a more productive avenue of representation. This broad solution will provide a transparent mechanism to represent concerns and suggest formal resolutions, which can be explained, articulated, and influentially presented. So far, shouting in the streets, the perception of anarchy, and the grumbling of disenchantment have provided us with diminished faith in our representation and little equitable resolution. On a micro level, legitimate social complaints have been exposed, publicly contemplated, and opaquely negotiated through the opinions of those with influence, concluding in divisiveness. But such divisiveness has relegated these issues to a minority status thereby quelling them and tucking them away without being appropriately addressed. The social impact of those issues may be immense, but they are deferred and made small by the lack of resolution. When only those with influence are given substantial ability to address an issue, they may predetermine or forge a resolution to suit their ambitions. By imposing inflated and deflated opinions they can opaquely divert public complaints, which end in stalemate and division. The minority with influence does not sufficiently address the perceived complaints of the majority without influence, which results in those without influence to be valueless. It is through dividing the valueless that the influential minority can maintain control and secure their comfortability. As a consequence of this divisiveness and lack of influence, individuals of the majority are inequitably exposed to an uncomfortable insecurity in their existence. Recognizing the strengths of the influential allows us to visibly pinpoint the specific problem and demand an appropriate solution. It is this feeling of being a valueless contributor that separates me, the individual, from the body that paints an unrecognizable portrait of my concerns and governs my conduct.

I tend to believe that the majority of the world population has the same gripe as mine. Many people, like me, have acquiesced to the perception made by the influential and governing few that those without power are valueless individuals. Until now, I have not understood that my being valueless has been derived through a nonrecognition of my influential rights. I have come to understand that the denial of these rights lay at the feet of the influential and their continuous pursuit toward authoritarianism. Many have fought for the scraps of the influential, misunderstanding the acquisition of materialism to be the only influential value, while their inborn right to an equitable influential value go unrecognized and therefore do not presently exist.

The idea that time and space constitute existence, and everything that exists has value, is a metaphysical concept. This concept has been examined and brought to practice in innumerable ways. That existence and consequently survival, mirrors raw influence, that value and consequently coexistence, mirrors material influence, is no fluke. Survival is a practical application, as is coexistence, the next step up in the chain of existence. It is important for us to apply sound metaphysical concepts to practical applications for the good of continued existence.

# 1.3.

## *Value and Fate*

IN 1865 THE THIRTEENTH AMENDMENT abolished slavery. Five years later, the Fifteenth Amendment prohibited federal and state governments from denying a person's right to vote based on "race, color, or previous condition of servitude." Beginning in 1870, four additional Amendments, enacted through a span of 101 years, concern the question of equality: the Fifteenth, Nineteenth, Twenty-fourth, and the Twenty-sixth. The Fifteenth addressed race, the Nineteenth addressed sex, the Twenty-fourth addressed civil credibility, and the Twenty-sixth addressed age.

The Constitution grants us our independent rights of liberty, belief, and expression. As incomplete as it may be, the Constitution grants us a measure of equality through the right to vote, and then applies the concept of representation as a means of protection and assurance, and then—bam! It stops right there. It doesn't allow for equal recognition of our value. Since the inception of the Constitution, pieces of equality have been granted, slowly and one at a time, as if implementing a conceptually pure democracy undergoes perpetual construction. God help us all if this is anything like road construction. If it is, we will never see equality fulfilled. Our right to equality is ensured by the guarantee of representation, and after 101 years of struggle our establishment suggests, by deferring discussion, that we have been provided with an appropriate measure of equality for all. But issues that concern influence constantly need to be addressed. The question isn't about existing equally. The question has been and still is the issue of protections. What protections toward the equality of influence do we have in our representation? The right to vote was always concerned with the equality of influence, and look at how many times that needed to be addressed. So exactly what is being protected by our representative's interpretations of present written law? The citizen's vote as a vocal exclamation of influence is being protected. No protections exist for the citizen's value as a material exclamation of influence. Without a material exclamation, equality of influence is unachievable. Both a material and a vocal exclamation are needed to fulfill an equality of influence. We have seen historical markers for those occasions such as those times when our representation has recognized protections ranging from color to sex to age, and yet we've struggled with the recognition of social economic barriers and social participation. The Twenty-fourth Amendment forbids the payment of any tax as a requirement to vote. Taxation is a measurable material exercise, and prior to the Twenty-fourth Amendment, the inability to perform that material exercise was cause to deny a citizen their vote. Material value and the inability to pay that value were used as denial to exercise vocal influence. Material value was recognized. Material value was used in law. So why wasn't an equitable measure of material value put into place as opposed to extracting the concept of material value from law, as it had unwittingly incorporated itself and needed to be removed through written constitutional doctrine? This feels like another historical marker to decidedly deny a form of equality and pacify the continued existence of inequality. By removing material influence and ensuring vocal influence, a decision was made to extinguish a light from exposing the truth, that material value has been recognized. Recognizing material value, the powers that be concealed its presence and new grand effort would be needed for it to be applied as a right. Looking back at the enactment of the Twenty-fourth Amendment, the powers that be could only claim oppression or complete ignorance in their absence to acknowledge material value. If asked today, I believe they would opt for ignorance and deny any effort to oppress. At the rate we've been going, it will be another 100 years before a few more slices of economic equality and recognition are addressed. It's ridiculous that it took 101 years to give all adults the right to vote. During this time, however, many people and groups have continued to maintain efforts to suppress greater measures of equality with the intent to secure control. We have had enough with these efforts of suppression. They are an affront to the people's right to economic equality and individual recognition.

Individual recognition within our social order should

be fully ensured by representation. But how does representation ensure the individual of recognition? Sure, our physical attributes have been recognized, but what about our social attributes? Our social existence is expected to contribute and generally does, but it still goes unrecognized. Our social existence is measured by the value we bring, and yet we've been assigned no recognizable value. We have no recognizable value because our potential goes unrecognized and yet, we insure our social contribution through or potential. Our individual potential exists as an unknown quantity. Our social potential exists as a known positive quantity. We know this by virtue of the sum of our continued contributions, efforts, and advancements to our society. If this were not true, we would still be living in caves knocking each other over the head with clubs, and civilization would not be occurring. We will gain validation for our contribution if our potential is recognized, and if our potential is recognized, then we provide proof of our value. When we gain the individual recognition of value in written law, our constitution will have finally addressed the equality of our social existence. Derived by the positive contribution of our potential, our social existence becomes an economic asset that requires the recognition of our value through a guarantee of economic equality.

Human rights reside in respecting the fundamental premise of freedom, equality, and recognition whereby any one of these cannot function without the other. Similarly, legal rights reside in respecting the fundamental premise of legislation, administration, and adjudication.

With regard to the constitutional checks and balances of our legal intercourse, one side cannot function without the other, and yet neither equality nor recognition has been fulfilled constitutionally. Presently, human rights in our democracy are partially functioning. The constitutional equality we presently possess lacks the recognition of our value. Without fulfilling equality and recognition, the function of freedom is incomplete! Those that are weighted with disproportionate distribution in society's organization understand this, as they live daily in its burden. Those who don't understand this may be enlightened through the examination of the distribution of education, which is not distributed equally. Recognition of its distributions is constantly debated. While this debate continues, poorly educated persons suffer a perceptual bond to servitude, which points to a deficiency of freedom—and the woeful state of education in this country is a national crisis affecting all segments of our society.

It is easier to visualize what has been happening by using a metaphor. In *Sabrina*, a wonderful film starring Audrey Hepburn and Humphrey Bogart, the chauffeur's daughter watches lavish parties from a tree. Eventually Sabrina comes down from the tree and joins the party. Through the course of our constitutional existence, different levels of equality have come down from the tree and joined the party. When Sabrina first joins the party, she is uncomfortable among a social group that has defined itself through wealth and sophistication. When race or sex or civil equality or age has joined the party, they have been uncomfortable among an established group that has defined itself through structured legal control. There's a scene in the movie when Linus, Humphrey Bogart's character, steals away from the party to a private area to discuss with his family how they will increase their stature. To a great degree, the discussion focuses on associations and marriage toward the goal of increasing their wealth and influence. They recognize value and then scheme to resource that value for their own purpose. We are now all invited to the party our establishment is hosting and, as we try to become comfortable among those in control, we see that they have recognized value and have stolen away to discuss their goals of possession and relinquishment of that value. By understanding the establishment's history, we feel their discussion is pertinent to how they can delay or avoid recognition of us and how they can get away with ignoring our value. They link influence to value and scheme to control influence for their own purpose. Like the only freshman at a senior dance, we are uncomfortable until we can associate equally and become recognized. When we become recognized for our value and have equal influence at this party that we have finally been able to join, we will become comfortable. The establishment will no longer be separated from us. We will become a contributing part of the establishment.

★   ★   ★

LET'S NOW FOCUS ON DETERMINING our value and, just

as important, let's identify which values each of us intrinsically possess and which values we experience or have as a result of day-to-day life. Potential is the one thing we all have in common throughout our existence. Our belief in potential contributes to the advancement of our societies. Potential gives us the ability to optimize opportunity. Potential cannot be discounted. If we were pessimists and flipped to the other side of the coin, we would see mankind with unpromising dread. If pessimism were the basis of our existence, mankind would not have advanced to this point. So it is potential that we rely upon in our growth, and it is potential that gives each one of us a predetermined value in our existence. We can logically designate that which is predetermined as original. So that we may differentiate our intrinsic values, we will state this predetermined value as our *original value*.

Although potential is a component to an individual's intrinsic value, it is only a small part. It's easiest to say that fate is the greatest component to one's intrinsic value. To be born into wealth or poverty, to be healthy or unhealthy, to lack or have intelligence, and to have good or bad fortune defines fate. Gaining or losing wealth, health, and intelligence becomes one's value. Utilizing efforts and turning opportunities into assets is not a foregone conclusion in the continuous adjustments of a person's value. Value derived from one's effort and one's fate is inequitable and it would make no sense to guarantee this as a component of equality. Each of us, regardless of our beliefs, must live our fate and accept the values that it may bring without an expectation for fate to guarantee equality. As a society, influence in our decision processes has relied upon material value derived through fate. It is individuals of great fortune and fate that have had the strongest influence, and individuals of the poorest fortune and fate that have had the weakest influence.

Those with good fate have been, and continue to be, fortunate to use their influence to secure the best odds of continuing good fate for themselves and their posterity. To address economic equality, we must put fate aside and focus on the *original value* of each citizen, securing the best odds of economic equality and recognition for themselves and their posterity. Through a constitutional amendment, the concept of *original value* can be materialized and applied as influence to secure that economic equality.

A Twenty-eighth Amendment would need to guarantee economic equality by recognizing a citizen's *original value*. It will need to monetarily identify each citizen's *original value* and recognize that value to be derived from society's collective provision of insurance through its citizen's potential. It will need to guarantee each citizen's *original value* by providing the insurance of representation. It will need to guarantee that the sum of the citizen's application of their *original value* can never be eclipsed by the sum of any other material values.

Having value is a derivative of being recognized and respected. In our American democracy we are fortunate to have our rights recognized and protected through our Constitution. Respect comes into question when we perceive our rights violated, stemming from that which we witness. If complete respect of the citizen's concerns is in any way diminished, then the citizen's value is diminished as well. That we can continue to fight for our rights is generally the focus, and we are fortunate to be able to have that fight. To deny or stall any discussion toward this proposal's concept and practical implementation would exacerbate economic inequality and indicate disrespect.

A politician and any individual seeking to represent others will always be searching for a way to offer value in return for a vote. Aside from obtaining a value offered, like addressing a particular concern, what other reason would anyone have to vote for a potential representative? Fulfillment by a representative of offers and promises made, of something deemed valuable, is another issue altogether. Of an offer, a promise, or a vote, only the vote contains value. It's a one-sided proposition. Promises and offers do not contain value; any weight of influence attached to them can be dismissed, and they can go unfulfilled. It is hollow to offer anything in return for a vote. The voter must rely upon full faith in the politician, which is impossible to have in every instance. Our relationship with politicians can lead to a greater degree of faith when the citizen's vote—their vocal exclamation— can be supported with a material exclamation: the implementation of their *original value*. The politician's respect of the citizen's concerns will require a greater degree of devotion and care and will provide an excuse for the politician to restrict or sever bonds that previously compromised the citizen's faith. Faith may be the greatest component missing in today's political representation, a component that can be restored through this proposal.

# 2.

## *APPLICATION*

# 2.1.

## *A Citizens Value*

WE COULD GO ON FOREVER merely discussing influence and it would make no difference. To make a difference, we must move beyond talk. We must put into place the "what" that is missing in our democracy: a citizen's constitutional right to influence. To convert our right to have influence into practice, we need to establish an equal material influence for each and every citizen. In order to do so, we must provide each and every citizen with a value. To affect decisions in our governance, a measurable Citizen's Value will need to be weighed against other material influences.

Establishing a Citizen's Value is easy. Its application, using it constructively and equating its value without eroding other assets that have created a profitable democracy, is the challenge. Common sense tells us that it will be necessary to establish an equal and uniform value for every citizen. Subsequently, its value can be integrated as a function of influence representing citizens' concerns.

First and foremost, a method to determine a Citizen's Value will get us started. While the entire population is different on any given day (given the perpetual fluctuation of births and deaths), using a method to come up with an average population count in a consistent way will have to be dictated. This is no different than methods that are used in a census to identify a specific population. After we establish the number of citizens, we'll need to establish an average value for each citizen. The combined declared gross income of all citizens, in the same year that we have used in our population census, should suffice for the equation. If we divide the population into the combined declared gross income, the resultant figure should do well to represent each Citizen's Value. An infant, a retired citizen, and every citizen in between will be represented with a value. At the end of the year prior to this writing, an estimation of Citizen's Value would have been approximately thirty thousand one hundred and fifty seven dollars ($30,157) per citizen. The purpose of this estimation is to illustrate function. We started with a population estimate of 324.3 million and a combined declared gross income of 9.78 trillion dollars.

If a Citizen's Value census was to be conducted annually, any variation of the assigned Citizen's Value figure should not change dramatically from year to year. Without the occurrence of a catastrophic event, say, a large and disproportional loss of lives or an eventful financial collapse, the change of both population and CGI (combined gross income) should not affect a Citizen's Value with great margin over a period of eight years. If an eight-year period is found to be sufficient between each Citizen's Value Census, then writing a strict clause and the terms to allow for an emergency census would permit for any necessary immediate revaluation between the designated censuses. A reasonable allotment of time will need to be coordinated for the two censuses, population and CGI, to be taken simultaneously. September 30 of the required year may be a good date for the censuses to be enumerated, recorded, and reported to establish or reestablish a Citizen's Value. This date will allow for preparation to conform to a new set of figures before January 1 of the following year, when the census information will come into effect. The first even year after a presidential election may work well for the census taking and reporting. Then the information from the census would be available to reestablish Citizen's Value outside of an election year. The only purpose a Citizen's Value Census serves will be to identify a monetary figure, a Citizen's Value, which will be used to represent every citizen. We will use $30,157 as our Citizen's Value. This will allow us to illustrate models of how, when, where and why the application of a Citizen's Value can and will be used.

★   ★   ★

THE REPRESENTATION OF INFLUENCE GAINED through the application of a Citizen's Value will come from the creation of an identity, a Citizen's Value Initiative, which will be legally permitted to channel citizens' material value, their donations, and nothing else. The rules involving such an identity must be created as a second section to the amendment, the first section identifying a

Citizen's Value. The purpose of this *instrument of representation*, a Citizen's Value Initiative, is to provide an entity that transfers material influence between the citizen population and their representation in government. The rules that define a Citizen's Value Allotment, the citizens legal use of material value toward their chosen Citizen's Value Initiative(s), how, how much and when, need to be discussed. The rules defining a Citizen's Value Initiative, how it is begun, how it ends, who can start it, how they can start it, where it must exist, how it handles its funds and how it is permitted to interact with government need to be logically thought through. A Citizen's Value is the primary topic, a Citizen's Value Initiative is a subtopic, and the interaction of Citizen's Value Allotments with representation in government is yet another topic. When these three units are defined separately, their rules and interactions will allow us to create a constitutional amendment that provides equality amongst citizens and a simple device to apply our civic responsibility. This will permit all citizens to have a direct, positive, and active influence in the function of their government.

The Internal Revenue Service will serve as an integral body for the transfer of Citizen's Value Allotments to Citizen's Value Initiatives. Oversight, accounting, recording of data, and the reporting of the consequential information in this interaction will be essential to transparency.

The IRS will be responsible to process, audit, and track the annual tax reports filed by citizens and from each of the legally registered Citizen's Value Initiatives. This will likely cause the IRS to create an independent body. Perhaps it could be called the IRS Department of Citizen's Value Administration (IRS–DCVA), with the ability of prosecutorial oversight including any misuse of funds by citizens, the Citizen's Value Initiative(s), and any illegal activity on the part of government representation.

Expenses incurred by the IRS–DCVA to function as a nonpartisan intermediary and provide accurate data will be provided from each Citizen's Value Initiative in equal amounts, regardless of any Citizen's Value Initiative's income. Part of the prerequisite to legally register, create, and maintain a Citizen's Value Initiative will require that the expense to the IRS–DCVA annual fee can be met. This will also require the IRS–DCVA to publish an annual expense report and set the Citizen's Value Initiative IRS–DCVA fee for the following year. The next chapter will go into greater explanation as to the interactions and functions of Citizen Value Initiatives.

★   ★   ★

THE RULES FOR THE USE of a Citizen's Value and procedurally, how and when it can be applied, how it is tracked and computed, who can apply it and precisely how every citizen can be represented are of topic now.

The time frame needed to conduct a Citizen's Value Census should not interfere with an annual report needed to identify how the citizens choose to apply their Citizen's Value Allotment. The time in which a citizen may donate their annual allotment will be any day of the year. Their donation will be recorded as part of their annual tax report provided to the IRS, who will in turn apprise the DCVA, which will calculate the Citizen's Value Allotments annually, making designated distributions with reporting of breakdowns. As part of its function, it will be necessary for the IRS–DCVA to transfer a citizen's designated funds at the time of their filing, if the citizen has not made that transfer independently. The IRS will then provide a comprehensive annual report on September 30, just in time for representatives to filter the information representing the nations concerns and prior to any election day.

The information provided to the IRS–DCVA needs to be guided by a few rules. The first concerns how a Citizen's Value Allotment is permitted to be used. In any given year, a Citizen's Value Allotment will be equal to the declared Citizen's Value, and no citizen may exceed their allotment. A Citizen's Value Allotment will begin January 1 and exhaust on December 31, annually, regardless of whether that allotment is used or not. Any unused allotments expire on December 31 of that year. The only stipulation to designate an application of funds from a Citizen's Value Allotment for the year in question will be a citizen's determination to donate funds that may be indicated in their annual IRS filing to which the IRS–DCVA will make that transfer. The Citizen's Value Allotment can only be used as a contribution toward any legally registered Citizen's Value Initiative(s). A citizen's total contribution(s) can be up to the full amount of their Citizen's Value of which they may contribute their allotment liberally to any legally registered Citizen's Value Initiative(s). When a citizen files their annual taxes, they will report the amount(s) of their contribution(s) correlated with the registered Citizens Value Initiative(s) they contributed to. Each Citizen's Value Initiative will have a registered identification code.

From the citizen's perspective this is the easy part. They contribute funds toward an initiative that they believe represents their concerns; they file the amount and then identify the initiative(s). Of course not everyone has funds to exhaust. While few citizens may have $30,157 to contribute, most other citizens may not. The function of this amendment is to provide an equitable measure of influence for all citizens. In the interest of equality and participation, a certain percentage of Citizen's Value should be expensed as a right. That the expense is equal for all citizens and that their right allows the citizen to have that expense with neither loss nor gain in the way it is accounted will be the measure of equality. To achieve neither loss nor gain, the expense will need to be recognized as its own entity. We will call this the Citizen's Value Equitable Allotment, or CVEA. We will designate one percent (1%) of a Citizen's Value as the CVEA. Although this percentage is debatable and can be set to that which is agreed, it is reasonable from many viewpoints, and it will allow us to move forward in this discussion. The CVEA, $301.57, will be deducted from gross income prior to any tax calculation for every citizen regardless of participation, making it fully deductible and nontaxable and equitable for all citizens. Further, to assure that any level of participation will neither increase nor decrease each citizen's net income, the CVEA should be accountable as a payment included with, and not separated from, the whole of taxes owed, should the citizen wish to participate. This provision in accounting, providing for neither monetary gain nor loss if one chooses nonparticipation, completely discounts the idea of this measure being identified as a tax. Other than the cost to administer this amendment, access to use these funds by government for its expenses will be off limits. Participation up to the full amount of a Citizen's Value, its disbursements, and designations are controlled by the citizen. The separation between government and the citizens in the use of these funds is visible, thus distinguishing it from a tax. If the CVEA, or any part thereof, is not claimed as donation to a Citizen's Value Initiative, then it will be collected as tax and used as the law has designated. This allows every citizen to participate.

As previously mentioned the importance of maintaining an influential balance in respect of all our democracy's assets leads us to discover another figure: the annual combined total income brought in by all legal entities permitted to donate and infuse their influence in the political arena, election committees, political action committees, party-affiliated committees, other organizations, and the like. To strike a balance in influence, one percent of Citizen's Value Allotments should exceed the funds brought in by these groups. If 1% of a Citizen's Value were designated as the tax-free portion, then it would be possible for the entire citizen population to contribute nearly $100 billion towards Citizen's Value Initiatives per year. This exceeds the annual amount that politically charged groups collectively infuse into our politics as of this writing.

When an amendment goes into effect honoring a Citizen's Value, the natural course of influence will dictate whether the citizen population will seek to eliminate, limit, or allow an overabundance to be maintained in regards to the present system of politically affiliated groups and their influence. While we will maintain for the benefit of all, that is, an interest in allowing the present system of influences in government, we must seek a framework that does not permit loopholes for any combination of material influences to ever exceed the citizen's material influence. It is important to recognize that the aspirations and exuberance of certain parties will always seek to create a greater influence representing their interests. It will become necessary as a part of doctrine to not permit these influences to exceed the citizen's influence in government. One of two methods can be used in order to maintain this balance. One method is designating a restriction to the total of material influences other than the citizens. This allows for the total value of citizens material influence to be designated at a stationary percentage. The other method, the use of a floating percentage representing a citizen's material influence would be cumbersome with greater difficulty to maintain and may permit lawmakers an easy way to adjust it to their benefit. This amendment can identify that; no other material influences combined totals can exceed the total sum of all Citizen's Value Equitable Allotment. Fairly and judiciously restricting the total funds from groups outside of this amendment will be the lawmaker's problem, as they have permitted its application in the first place. This allows us to apply a stable percent of Citizen's Value, the CVEA, to be deducted from claimed gross income tax-free and accounted for as a part of total taxes owed, realized as influence, with neither monetary gain nor loss for every citizen. In any case that the deduction from taxes owed results in a negative figure, that negative figure will automatically convert to zero dollars. In no way will the government or any of its entities pay a monetary figure to any citizen or Citizen's Value Initiative as a part or whole claim of Citizen's Value.

So now what about the other 99% of a Citizen's Value? If 1% of Citizen's Value is deducted and tax-free, the remaining amount, $29,855.43 will be taxable, nondeductible and not accounted as any part of payment to taxes owed. Citizens may still contribute to any Citizen's Value Initiative(s) and express their concerns in excess of the CVEA. Any portion of 99% of a Citizen's Value still remains to be used if one wishes to do so.

The application of common law, as it is understood today, will be the guideline for each citizen's representation in the application of their Citizen's Value. An infant, in the first day of life, will be represented by their guardian, as will be any person with a legal designation to guardianship. It is important to note that any citizen whose legal guardian is the government will not have their representation in the Citizen's Value program nullified. In every case in which a citizen's legal guardian is the government, then 1% of citizen's value will be mandatorily distributed equally among every legally registered Citizen's Value Initiative for that year, until such time that the government is no longer there guardian.

# 2.2.

## *A Citizen's Value Initiative*

IN THE DOCUMENTATION FOR A constitutional amendment we must address three things:

- How a "Citizen's Value Initiative" can be created, sustained, and dissolved and by whom and under what terms it is permitted to exist
- How it addresses and identifies its concern, defining the confines or extension of that concern and how it can be permitted, or whether it should be permitted at all, and, if necessary, to redefine the concern
- How it will present itself publicly and how it is permitted to interact with elected and appointed representatives in government

For a Citizen's Value Initiative to become a reality, a formidable level of study and negotiation will be necessary if we want to see this imitative written with precision as the law of the land. As for my contribution to this endeavor, I write to build, not hone, the mechanisms that will allow this proposal to be envisioned in its entirety. I am holding an antique pocket watch. As I examine its beautiful exterior and admire this device's precision and accuracy to tell time, I am reminded of the working vision I have of a Citizen's Value. They both possess magnificence, a truth in reality, and a smooth consistency to perform their tasks. I visualize the mechanisms inside this timepiece and grasp the calculation and accuracy needed for these springs and gears and clips and clasps to help each in their function and operate smoothly. I see a Citizen's Value Initiative in the same way. I am but one individual attempting to bring a concept to life, a concept so grand that its refinement will require many people from all walks of life to converge upon it, to study, question, calculate, and build its function.

## 2.2.1. Creation to Termination

THIS CHAPTER EXPLAINS THE PRACTICAL implementation to the idea of citizens asserting their influence through the application of a citizen's value, which is derived through their potential and is recognized as a Constitutional right to individual possession of original value.

A Citizens Value Initiative, when created, will be a mechanism by which a citizen can apply any portion of their Citizen's Value Allotment. This designated application of allotment by the citizen transfers funds into the CVI(s) of their choice. A CVI, by virtue of their declared purpose, will represent a specific view or opinion of a concern. Each CVI created will be an "instrument" representing citizens supporting the perspective of a concern to which the citizen has designated their donation. Each CVI will be supported by donation solely derived from each citizen's designation from their Citizen's Value Allotment. With appropriate laws, a CVI can function relatively the same as existing entities permitted to apply influence in government. A citizen's view, supported by donation of their allotment, will be represented through the mechanism of a CVI, which will be permitted direct contact with government representatives. A CVI's explicit purpose is to influence government with respect to their declared specific concern. The particular details regarding who, how, why, where, and when of a CVI are discussed in this chapter.

An expectation of thousands of Citizen's Value Initiatives will be created to address the multiple viewpoints of hundreds, and perhaps thousands, of concerns. To be attentive of where the responsibility and liability resides, it makes sense that only one citizen should be the creator and principal of any individual CVI. The individual's time and dedication used to maintain their legal obligations in operation of their CVI will be provided for, given that the intended structure will permit them an income. A restriction that prevents any one individual to create and operate more than one CVI at the same time will avoid immoderation to mingle multiple initiatives and allow the principal to focus on accomplishing the CVI's concern. While a group of citizens with the same objective may coordinate to create multiple CVIs in order to achieve a goal common among them, they will find that multiple

CVIs may actually dilute focus and strength toward their purpose. Collecting their eggs in one basket may prove to make a bigger omelet feeding a larger purpose.

A CVI proving its success by continued citizens donations, and remaining sustainable over a period of time, may find the necessity to have an operating staff. The structure of this amendment should permit both the principal and any staff an appropriate wage. With economic transparency as to the CVI's activity and a restriction in this amendment to the amount of payroll distribution that is permissible, the donating citizen can be reassured that they are not financing a personal expedition of greed. It would not be unreasonable to use the IRS annually published figure—the average individual annual income of the American citizen—which can be used to set the livable income of a staff employee to a CVI. That being said, one and one-half times that figure would be neither underpaid nor overpaid for the principal. The purpose of a CVI, to represent a concern of the citizens, makes setting proportional payroll figures relevant so as to not make a CVI available as a private get-rich scheme.

If thousands of CVIs are permitted to be created, it will be helpful for all parties seeking information to categorize the CVIs. Our representatives in government delve into so many issues. Segregating those issues and attaching descriptions or perspectives to a category may be presumptive and inaccurate at the onset. Perhaps it is best to allow a free flow of categorizations to build naturally as the process of CVI creations occur. Publication of the identity and purpose of each CVI as they are created will be more relevant than presuming our ability to categorize. I would propose that all CVIs and only CVIs be entitled to .cvi, similar to .com, .org or .gov, as identification on the Internet. This can be of great value in creating, formatting, categorizing, and maintaining transparency in the construction and ongoing use of this proposed amendment.

The IRS Department of Citizen's Value Administration will be needed to administer the business from creation to termination of all CVIs. This system we're creating would distill a citizen's potential to recognize their material value, and then transfers their material value to an influential value. Regardless of the conceptual transferences, the citizen is essentially implementing money and transferring it to gain political influence. Since the activity of a CVI revolves around money and entails financial transparency, a form will need to be designed for reporting to the IRS–DCVA. This form, the CVI Annual Declaration, will necessitate CVIs to identify the bodies they conduct interactions with and make the correlating financial declarations. Categorizing, enumerating, and reporting the connections and financial activities of citizens, CVIs and the entities they administer business with will become available to the IRS through the collection of our individual tax report, this CVI Annual Declaration and tax reports required for businesses. This may compel the IRS to provide line item declarations on business tax forms relative to this proposal.

The cost to taxpayers in the administration of this proposed amendment should be derived through the

CVIs. In general terms, the amendment will need to recognize the cost to CVIs in the application of their business including payroll, rent, operating overhead, project expenses, travel, etc. The legitimacy of a CVI's expenses will be borne through the transparency of their financial reporting. This disclosure made public then falls into the hands of the donating citizens for investigation. Given that the CVIs will be required to finance the administration of this amendment, any CVI unable to do so will need to be terminated without question. A popular and well-donated CVI will find no difficulty in their equal obligation to the IRS–DCVA for the cost of overall administration.

If anybody can go out and start a CVI for whatever their cause may be, without requirements during initiation, then we will invite absolute and pure insanity. To initiate and register a CVI with the IRS Department of Citizen's Value Administration, the principal should meet standards that display both their dedication and the dedication of a volume of citizens desiring to support that CVI's registered purpose. To be definitive and to avoid miscommunication, this will mean that the same declared purpose of the CVI is exposed to the IRS and to any citizen invited to donate to the creation of that CVI. This can be accomplished by submitting a CVI preregistration form to the IRS–DCVA declaring a principal, a name, and the purpose of the CVI. This same form will be required to legitimize any citizen at the time of their endorsement toward the creation of the CVI.

Recognizing a citizen's dedication and deciding upon

the necessary volume of citizen support to initiate a CVI will rely upon a few factors. Any citizen willing to support a CVI during its creation should be required to dedicate their entire Citizens Value Equitable Allotment in the year of creation, approximately $300. As well, their signature as endorsement will be required on the same preregistration form initially submitted to the IRS–DCVA. At such time that a predesignated volume of citizens endorsements are collected, the proposed CVI can resubmit the preregistration as an endorsed registration for creation. Once the endorsed registration is approved by the IRS–DCVA, the CVI can begin to conduct business.

But hold on! Where are they going to get their money to start conducting business? Before we get to that, we need to find the appropriate volume of citizen endorsements required to create a CVI. A few criteria should be understood to approximate the volume of citizens needed, such as an estimate of the annual administration cost owed to the IRS as well as an estimate of initial overhead, payroll, and operating expenses of an average CVI and an estimate of the volume of CVI's to be created or operating in a single year. This may seem like throwing a dart at the side of a barn to get realistic numbers but we will have to start somewhere. After a few years from ratification, this proposed amendment will see the real numbers and will have to adjust. For the time being, we understand the IRS total budget to be in the neighborhood of $13 billion for 2017. So let's say that the IRS–DCVA will need an annual budget of $8 billion and we approximate 2,000 CVI's to be created in the initial year.

Each CVI would then need to expense $4 million toward administration. If we expect a CVI to meet an average annual expense in overhead and operations of $3 million, then the CVI should be making ends meet at $7 million. Giving room for the CVI to conduct business, the combined total from each endorsing Citizen's Value Equitable Allotment should amount to twice that of all the criteria combined. This means the CVI should begin doing business with a donated annual income of $14 million. Per our earlier estimate of the CVEA, it would take endorsements from 46,667 citizens at approximately $300 each to accumulate the $14 million need to create and sustain a CVI in its first year. Given this reckoning, we would be best served at establishing the volume of citizen endorsements required to create a CVI at 50,000. Although it may be possible, I hardly think that the principal would want to travel door to door to get 50,000 signatures. It will have to be determined by the individual seeking to create a CVI as to how they will accomplish that goal. With the use of the Internet and social media, I am sure that many people will figure out how to appropriately implement newer technology to properly accomplish the endorsement portion required for creation. Regardless, each endorsing citizen's signature, and proof of that, will need to be mandatory.

To understand this clearly, a citizen may seek help and funding from other citizens, foundations, and organizations to preregister with the intention to create a CVI. That same help may continue until the point that an endorsed registration for creation is submitted to the IRS–

DCVA. In this process of preregistration nothing should be assumed; therefore, protections would need to be put into place to avoid those that would seek to undermine the pure intention of this pursuit. As an obvious example, giving people money, material goods, or favors for their endorsement will be illegal. It is unfortunate I have to mention that which should be presumed and respectfully accorded as common sense. Nevertheless, precisely at the time that the CVI's registration is approved by the IRS–DCVA, the CVI will no longer be permitted to accept funding from any other source than the Citizen's Value donations as prescribed in this amendment. This enables citizens to begin or continue their pursuits and at the time of CVI approval, disenfranchise material ties with sources outside this proposal. In this way, economics becomes incorporated in the concept of individual equality. This institutionalizes the concept of individual influence and economic equality for every citizen, guaranteed by the Constitution.

We now have an endorsed citizen's commitment to be collected by the IRS–DCVA when all the requirements are fulfilled for the creation of a CVI. At this point the IRS–DCVA will be required to transfer $14 million into a bank account established by and for the CVI. A provision to recapture the IRS–DCVA annual administration fee expensed during the initiation will be made. During this process the IRS–DCVA will assign an identification code to the CVI that will be implemented for all their activities, including its financials and bank account. The CVI should be restricted to maintaining one account for all its activities keeping transparency and reporting simple.

Nearly $100 billion annually can be dedicated by this amendment to a structure that provides economic equality and individual influence for every citizen in the nation. This is certainly an adequate figure to fund oversight, support and enforcement, conduct business, and fairly influence political representation so that the fabric woven comes from the fiber of the nation. In no way should this proposal to amend the Constitution be seen as a legitimized competition for influence by throwing money around. This is to propose that the citizen's rights come before, and above, and beyond, the rights of any legal institution previously existing, or to come into existence, for the purpose of influencing political outcomes. Political action committees immediately come into mind. While the courts have found their legitimacy with a determination in favor of the purpose they serve, they and any other institutions' funds contributed toward any political format should be considered a form of material influence. This proposed amendment needs to contain language that enforces all three branches of government to recognize any total conglomeration of material influence from sources outside of this amendment. By government recognizing that monetary sum, and as a protection to the American citizen, I reiterate that this amendment will need to mandate that monetary totals of material influence will be restricted to never exceed the annual monetary sum of the citizens CVI contributions. Nothing is a guarantee in life. For centuries we have seen the guarantees of our Constitution manipulated, contested, defined, and redefined. We know that attempts made to maximize influence will seed new contrivances that must be protected against, just like protecting against those with the idea that "you're not trying hard enough, if you're not cheating." While this amendment attempts to guarantee economic equality, it will be challenged no differently than any other. That being said, it is certainly a concept that comes closer to any presently known in the fight for economic equality.

## 2.2.2. Identification and Definition

THE INSTRUMENT OF REPRESENTATION, A Citizen's Value Initiative, must be constrained in multiple ways. Its purpose, to voice and express the concern initiated by contributing citizens, must maintain a responsible performance toward expressing the concern of its existence. However, a long-winded declaration of a CVI's goals and purpose should be avoided. It will be in no one's interest, especially the donating citizen, to have to read a book to understand what is proposed and what they expect to achieve. Nor will it be of any help for a protracted declaration to include an overwhelming volume of proposals and goals. It would be like declaring, "The purpose of this CVI is to achieve world peace," which is a wonderful thought. However, many books or one huge tome would need to be written to describe the step-by-step purpose and procedure of how a CVI could actually achieve world peace. The declaration of a CVI will be best served as a short proclamation, 50 words or fewer to identify the purpose and goal intended of any CVI. As CVI's are created and terminated a natural filtering will occur. This filtering will lead to a healthy defining and redefining of the issues and their relevance.

Naturally, complete transparency of each CVI's purpose, goals, identity, and economics will be mandatory. This will allow, from all viewpoints, citizens and representatives to understand the specific nature of a CVI and what they hope to gain. Should a CVI be permitted, even slightly, to refocus its purpose? Primarily, the answer lies with the responsibility it had assumed upon creation to its citizen donors. Should it happen that a CVI is permitted to readjust its focus, it will mean slighting the citizen's concern from its origination. In the aspect of maintaining credibility to those who believe in a concern they have donated to, it will be best to not allow a CVI to change whatsoever its declaration of purpose at origination. For whatever reason, if a CVI seeks to change its purpose, then it will need to pursue the course of terminating itself and initiating the creation process from the beginning with its new purpose.

While any CVI's concern should be permitted to liberally expose itself, a confinement to its stated purpose should be reinforced as a protection to the contributing citizens. To achieve this reinforcement, each CVI will need to make all of their past, present, and future activities publicly available at any time. The activities would be defined separately as follows: individual interactions, group interactions, and financial interactions. All interaction activities should include contacts, meetings, discussions, advertisements, and contributions. Any contact, and/or discussion by an individual or group with any government representative, opponent, or advocate would be an interaction and should require a complete and transparent publication. Individual and group interactions including private contacts should require exposure as to the content of such meetings. In addition, group interactions would require the same exposure to include a record-keeping volume indicating the level of participation. Financial activities should include the number of donors, the volume of contributed income, and all disbursements itemized, which would include contributions and their specifics.

With respect to a CVI, we have expressed the word "concern" singularly so that we may identify any CVI's purpose and goal specifically. Each CVI representing a singular concern permits us, after enumeration, to understand its identity and its degree of influence by virtue of the populace contributing to that concern. A CVI advocating the liberal concern of a particular issue can be weighed against another CVI advocating a conservative perspective of the same concern. In the regard to many common day dilemmas, a CVI may present its concern with a plausible solution that has not been previously considered. Solutions that had been disregarded without malice or foresight will certainly be deliberated by the common enterprise of the citizens. I predict that the nature of our citizen's collaborations will return stunning results offering new solutions. Presently, reliance upon polling and opacity as to the independent nature and motives of the pollsters and publishers provides us with uncertain and biased presumptions and resultant arguments to many issues of the day.

Specificity and constraint to the purpose of a CVI, having a fixed and narrow focus, will likely be critical to a CVI's success. A CVI's declaration of its specific purpose will permit the grouping of concerns of multiple CVIs and will serve to spotlight priorities by virtue of their citizen's participation. Multiple CVIs can be created to address aspects of a common larger concern and by virtue of declaring a fixed focus; the micro concerns of these CVIs can be put into proportion, organized, and daisy-chained to find resolution(s) of the larger concern.

CVIs can be created to address broader concerns through declaring all the aspects of that concern to be their sole purpose. However, that CVI may find great difficulty in prioritizing and creating recognition for some or all aspects of that broader concern. For instance, a CVI can be created with its declaration. "The purpose of this CVI is to pass legislation that guarantees all information provided from any source will be accurate." While the broad scope and vague intent of such a purpose may permit the CVI to dabble with many issues relative to the presentation of information or sources or accuracy, it does not allow the donating citizen to understand its specific goal. CVIs will learn how to accomplish their goals. The concept, to sustain its existence until it has achieved its purpose, will be realized. If a purpose has been achieved by the citizens, then the CVI will have exhausted its usefulness and will proceed to termination. We may find that support for an aged and sustained CVI declaring a broad purpose today may be the impetus for micro-focused CVIs to successfully find solutions to pieces of that broad purpose in the future. In this respect, it is plausible that a number of CVIs will be created with broad focus and will be sustained over a long period of time. It is likely that the nature of these CVIs will be pertinent to issues for which we have long struggled to find a solution. However protracted, this will be a healthy discourse towards finding eventual solution to a few of our most troubling issues.

While I am hesitant to express my personal opinions on any specific concern, I will attempt to discuss a particular one without bias and provide examples of how that concern may be approached through the use of CVIs. Because the relevance of information influence is an aspect and component inherent to this proposal, I will describe some micro and broadly focused initiatives and their goals as they relate to information.

A "News Label" CVI may be created with its declaration, "The purpose of this CVI is to pass legislation stating that extraneous information published or broadcast and labeled as 'news' will be liable as to that information's truth and accuracy and that the publisher or broadcaster of false information can be prosecuted for perjury."

A "False News" CVI may be created with its declaration, "The purpose of this CVI is to pass legislation permitting the publisher and broadcaster of any information, commentary, advertisement, or editorial to have no liability as to that information's truth and accuracy whatsoever."

A "Source News" CVI may be created with its declaration "This CVI's purpose is to pass legislation permitting the publisher and broadcaster of any information to be void of liability as to the truth and accuracy of that information provided they specifically declare the source of that information simultaneously with and during its publication or when it is broadcast."

A "Fake News" CVI may be created with its declaration "The purpose of this CVI is to pass legislation requiring licensed publishers and or broadcasters of any information to specifically label that information as 'Fiction' or 'Nonfiction' at the time of its publication."

An "Information Liability" CVI may be created with its declaration "The purpose of this CVI is to pass legislation requiring any transmission of information by any entity, regardless of intention, to be labeled as 'Fiction' or 'Nonfiction' with prosecutorial liability residing with the transmitter."

A "Constitutional News Right" CVI may be created with its declaration "The purpose of this CVI is to insure that no legislation can or will be passed governing news, citing full enforcement of the First Amendment of the United States Constitution, that 'Congress shall make no law…'."

As any of these examples of CVI's gains momentum as a result of increased contributions, we will see a specific focus toward a majority resolution. When the purpose of any CVI become irrelevant, citizens will redirect their contributions, causing that initiative to fizzle and exhaust its existence.

The following statement is my opinion: I would hope that our nation would influence our representation to recognize that labeling news is not an infringement "abridging the freedom of speech, or of the press" provided such labeling is used only to hold the news provider accountable to its accuracy. It is my estimation that any identification tag, whether it be fact or opinion or advertisement or fiction or nonfiction would be of great help to society in general, especially in times when some representatives in government routinely present information that, as a result of fact checking, is often found inaccurate by means of omissions, distortions, vague inaccuracies, and outright lies.

For durability's sake, it will be incredibly helpful to understand proportionality in setting goals for an achievable purpose at the creation of a CVI. While it will be legally entitled, a CVI with a broad declaration and purpose will likely find itself stuck in the same quagmire that presently exists in today's political atmosphere leading to disenchantment and a loss of public interest. If our governing representatives realize that multiple CVIs address similar concerns, citizens will need to weed out CVIs by their relevance and leave popular and well-funded CVIs time for greater recognition of their specific concern. This sustained period during which it is recognized that multiple CVIs address similar concerns will allow for a melding of the issues and an opportunity to identify solutions to the general concern in question.

Ultimately, and with patience, citizens, by virtue of their application of material influence, will be of great help to their representatives in government. Upon initiation of this proposed amendment it should not be expected that the concerns would be identified and addressed immediately by our representation. However, after the initial years of application and ongoing use of this amendment, representation will find a continuous and up-to-date flow of incredibly valuable information relevant to their constituency, which should be highly regarded in their decision process.

With all of the different issues that the nation's citizens may wish to address, an assortment of viewpoints will be stated by multiple CVIs on behalf of their concern. Some CVIs, created to influence their opinions of more personal concerns, will undoubtedly be counteracted. In a close contest, no action by government representatives may be the best approach. If those personal concerns are of a great interest to a body of citizens, then those CVIs may endure generations before their opinions and concerns are approachable for resolution. Some CVIs may be created to address concerns of a civic nature such as attempting to distinguish a balance between privatization or government control of communal infrastructures. Even in this regard, the citizen's influence may be of great help to situations that are presently addressed through the courts. Citizen's material expression of influence will help administrative, legislative, and judicial entities identify resolutions in common with the citizen's plea. It will consistently be the material influence of a "Citizen's

Value" through a "Citizens Value Initiative" which will expose concerns, bring discussion, and find resolution in the short or long-term.

## 2.2.3. Presentation and Interaction

THE WAY IN WHICH A "Citizen's Value Initiative" may present its concern should be liberally decided by that CVI. It would be impossible to fathom the creativity, today and in the future, of the extent and manner of which a CVI can express its influence. There are a few ways to achieve its goal: a CVI may wish to publish written copy, purchase advertising space, donate to political campaigns, donate to experimental not-for-profits seeking solutions to their concern, schmooze with representatives in government, initiate legal proceedings, and organize marches or protests. This does not mean that a CVI will have an à la carte free-for-all with a citizen's donations and ignore the influence it is expected to initiate and sustain. It will be a consistently visible method or procedure along with a citizen's oversight to decipher legitimacy in the widespread nature of its expenditures. A CVI that donates to an experimental not-for-profit that is seeking a solution to its concern is a good example of an expenditure that should be intricately examined by those making the donation. The CVI's activities will reveal if the experimental not-for-profit's operation is personally connected or in any way returns a profit to the executives, administrators, or any other persons for their personal embellishments. Any CVI leaving information undisclosed and creating opacity of its behavior should be temporarily suspended and frozen, investigated, and upon conviction of nondisclosure, mandatorily terminated with consequence to the principal, including punishment.

There's no doubt that "schmoozing with representatives in government" is an attention getter. To put all our minds at ease, constructing language to make illegal the transfer of any sum of money from the CVI to any individual will be included. Restricting a CVI from providing funding to businesses, both public and private, will also be necessary. Permitting a CVI the ability to donate to political campaigns should also require language restricting the principal from running for or holding an elected or appointed public office. Language defining a CVI's affiliation, interactions, and restrictions to religious organizations will have to be entered upon. Limitations and lucid methods of contact will need to be applied so that citizen's recognize a legitimate business atmosphere between the CVIs and government representatives.

Without a doubt, a CVI's permitted interactions will take the greatest consideration when writing law.

Entering into what a CVI can and cannot do with the money it receives will be a ticklish debate. At the onset, mimicking the rules of organizations that are legally permitted political intercourse allows a citizen to achieve balance in today's overall structure. I believe this would suffice as influence deserved by citizens. Furthermore, if a balance of influence in our political structure is achieved, this will guarantee economic equality, and so nothing more would be needed. Some will go further by calling for a broader expression of rights to be permitted, to which caution should be observed. Congress will be responsible for writing these laws, and a keen examination of what they produce will be necessary. A public insisting that their value be realized will be part and parcel of a broad Constitutional Amendment, to which I am more confident, and less concerned with reliance upon our representation.

Government representatives all conduct business in locations relative to their responsibilities and constituency. This may include the state they represent, the state of their residence, or the nation's capital. By restricting a CVI's contact with a government representative to solely those locations, we condense the business at hand to a business location.

We will need to allow a CVI the extension to roam about in order to make contact *or* to declare a singular location of business with satellite offices. Individuals representing the CVI will need to travel, but there is no reason to permit those individuals to meander at the expense of the donating citizen. The interest and purpose of any given CVI may dictate that it is best located in the nation's capital and needs no other satellite offices. The needs of a different CVI may require satellite offices in locations more pertinent to its cause, perhaps in one state or a few states or all the states. By permitting CVIs no more than 51 offices, one as their declared location and 50 satellite offices available, no more than one in each state, we then provide a connection by location between the CVI and government representatives. A restriction allowing contact only in locations designated by state or the nation's capital common to both the representative and the CVI permits business to be conducted without an overabundance of travel. This certainly helps remove some luxury destinations from the "schmooze." Allowing CVIs to maintain satellite offices grants the opportunity for those CVIs to invite government representatives to locations for purposes of demonstration. Concerns may be best expressed at locations that demonstrate a relevant impact. Environmental, business, immigration, potential disaster, etc., are not limitations to using a location to get the message across. Again, it is citizen oversight that recognizes an abuse initiated by a CVI. A CVI with a declared purpose of creating legislation toward maintaining, protecting, and restoring coastal beaches but happens to have a satellite office in a Rocky Mountains ski resort may have some explaining to do. It will be up to the citizens to continue their donations or not.

To be sure, many Americans with the intention of creating a CVI would love to do nothing less than pester the heck out of government representatives. Little good will come of this if any CVI structures itself as an annoyance. Regardless, a CVI should have the ability to contact government representation without being denied that contact and, respectively, government representatives should have the ability to turn down any CVI at any time for whatever reason they deem necessary. To satisfy both sides in the manner in which contact can be made, each government representative should be mandated to personally meet at least once each year with every CVI that has invited the representative to meet. In so much as we should expect the schedule of a government representative to be more stringent than that of the CVI, we should allow the government representative to decide the time and location of any such meetings, restricted to common locations as previously discussed. Furthermore, so that any CVI is impeded from causing any trouble, we should contain the volume of invitations a CVI can make to each representative in each year. For every invitation that is made, the government representative should be required to respond. Their response to accept or deny any invitation should be published along with the details of time and location upon acceptance. In this way, the citizens can witness the conduct and interaction between the government representative and the CVI that wishes to express its purpose and goal. The same transparency mandated for all CVIs would need to be mandated for the people, organizations, and government representatives that the CVI makes contact with. Understandably, time frames would need to be implemented with respect to responses and scheduling of such invitations so that either party is not given the opportunity to blow it off.

To go a step further, government representatives who wish to meet with CVIs should be viewed as a promising intention to understand all of the CVI's purpose and goals. While the CVI may have the privilege to deny contact with a government representative, that would be averse to accomplishing their goal. Therefore, we should allow government representatives to contact and meet with CVIs at their whim for whatever purpose or clarification they wish to engage in. That such meetings would be published with the time, the location, the people and the content should be sufficient for the onlooking public. As it is the intention of this amendment to influence government representation into making decisions in favor of and for the good of the populace, any communication requested from government representation should not be denied.

In the very sense that occurrences of material influence guide decisions at the local and state levels, an allowance for CVIs to contact all three levels of government, while respecting previously mentioned restrictions, should be allowed. It is neither uncommon nor implausible for local or state governments to find solutions to both simple and complex social issues. Ultimately, lower levels of government instituting new resolutions brought forth from CVIs allow an appropriate testing ground for the common good. In the entirety of the citizen concerns to be addressed, those concerns should be permitted to saturate all levels of government.

Any municipality or state that wishes to implement all or a part of this concept in their bylaws or Constitution would be instituting an acknowledgment of their citizens' value and would create economic equality in their community. Any group of people, any nation, anywhere in the world will find their adversities and equality acknowledged by successfully demanding their material value to be recognized and respected. All nations recognizing and respecting their citizens' value will, in eventuality, unite the world in peaceful economic equality.

Tactics of suppression and the use of influence will consistently seek to deny the success of this concept. In its most obvious form, suppression by virtue of physical harm, confinement, and the like will be utilized by governments and government entities in fear of losing their domination. Other forms of suppression, like invalidating information, or presenting it with misrepresentations, omissions, and falsifications will be the tools consistently used by influence brokers in today's America. It should be expected that a minority class, anywhere in the world, of the most powerful individuals would not easily relinquish their manipulation of influence. Driven by a desire of supremacy, this class will afford many different avenues toward maintaining control and using techniques of suppression to deny any concept enabling the citizen population a platform of equal influence. For those with something to hide and the appropriate means to do so, it has become commonplace to utilize material influence toward misrepresenting and/or suppressing exposure of the hidden. This has become another example of tactical suppression. It is time for economic equality to be used to influence the direction of democracy. No longer should any citizen, or group of citizens, acquiesce to any form of suppression.

The subject of suppression should be, and may very well be, the closing chapter of this proposal. Tactical suppression and its contrivances will likely be exploited by those who want to portray nonexistent negative aspects of a Citizen's Value and the initiatives that will assert the citizens representative influence. It will be one thing to question and seek solutions. It will be something entirely different to say *no*! Those expected contrivances, as a reflection of their creators, will reveal their ambitions by seeking to find ways in which to discredit this concept of Citizen's Value. Others, searching for ways this proposal can be manipulated to an evil end, will help to recognize necessary caution. I invite their candor.

Over time our Constitution has taught us that good decisions will prevail. So it will be that jurisprudence will, like so many previous constitutional arguments, find the intentions of a Citizen's Value in favor of equality "of the people, by the people and for the people." It is in this idea and the acceptance of this concept that good will prevail over evil.

# 2.3.

## *A Citizens Value Rendered*

REPRESENTATION MADE THROUGH A BALANCED utilization of influence and executed with regard to a citizen's concerns is the goal of instituting a Citizen's Value amendment. All is for not, if representation chooses to ignore citizens' concerns. Our government's represent-atives are elected by the citizens, and so the Citizen's Value proposal is one that will primarily be influenced by citizens. The reaction to this proposal by our elected officials will no doubt remove any question as to a representative's loyalty, faith, motives and goals in their responsibilities.

Should this proposal initiate construction and ratifica-tion of an amendment, we need to lay out our expectations in practical terms. Most people will expect Citizen's Value Initiatives to be born out of concern for our most common issues of the day, and they will not be wrong. We will see CVIs created to influence perspectives of existing Constitutional Amendments, including this proposal as an Amendment. We'll see CVIs directed towards all issues of law. We will see CVIs concerned with aspects of business, social and personal matters. We will see CVIs interested in implementing strategies of religious orientation, personal identity, environmental awareness, international relations, ethics of every degree and rung on society's ladder, and so much more. If anyone of us can formulate a reasonable complaint, offer a reasonable solution from our perspective, and gain reasonable support, we can create a CVI to influence recognition of our concern. We shouldn't be surprised to see activists of every sort making a go at creating a CVI. We shouldn't be surprised at some absurdities that will seek to be recognized through forming a CVI. I have often wondered why businesses utilizing public roads as temporary parking aren't required to register and pay a small annual fee to local, county, or state authority for that utilization. Other businesses incur costs to provide parking. These businesses congest the roadways and profit at the expense of the taxpayer. That I can only create one CVI will not enable me to pursue my absurd hissy little attitude toward other businesses and their use of community infrastructures. However, if this were my only concern and it kept me up all night and I couldn't let it go, I would be within my rights to pursue the creation of a CVI to address this issue. We will be surprised when some concerns that seem minute and not worthy of public scrutiny gain support. People will see what others are thinking and can privately decide to act upon their own thoughts and opinions.

Reports will expose statistical numbers of citizens' support and provide clarity as to the activities of all the CVIs. The privacy to support a CVI of one's choosing will need not be exposed other than our annual IRS filing. The right to privacy must be, and will be, respected.

We should expect to see advertisements by CVIs seeking donations from Citizen's Value Allotments, exposing their concerns, complaining, pointing the finger, and bad-mouthing everything on the planet. We should expect CVIs to be created seeking legislation toward restrictions aimed at complaining, bad-mouthing and finger-pointing. Heck, we already have complaining, finger-pointing and bad-mouthing. Maybe we'll see what everyone thinks about it and finally do something about it. We should expect all the grievances of today to be laid on the table, aired out, organized, prioritized, and addressed sequentially as their degree of importance is unveiled.

We will see every scheme imaginable used by CVIs to express their concerns and gain momentum. The only restriction to one or more schemes may be that which is written into law as part of this amendment. Restricting a scheme may be a sticking point in that our representatives will be writing the law. Because it's a fact that representatives have a history of dragging their feet when it comes to recognizing equality, the citizens of our nation must be cognizant of the language our representatives will choose to use in the writing of any laws pertinent to this proposed amendment. The construction of the amendment itself must seek language that defines and prevents lawmakers from enabling restrictions for today and future generations. As an example, discussion by our representation towards this proposal may lead to agreement that CVIs should not be permitted to donate to political campaigns. I believe that any restriction, relative to a subject that been granted infusion of other influences, would display inequality. As far as schemes go and what a CVI may do, it is hard to imagine that they can do something that has not already been done by other organizations with material and political influence. That being said, human creativity brings what can be imagined closer to reality as time passes.

We will become more intimate with our representatives, thereby giving us a detailed look at their motives and interactions with their cronies. Any perception that a representative's personal concerns and wealth are paramount should dissipate as a sense of faith is restored. This perception is not a reflection of every individual in representation; however, the power given permits clouded motives to permeate the decisions made in light of personal versus citizens' concerns and resonates as a problem that presently plagues our democracy. This increased intimacy between citizen and representative, from local to national arenas, will help many citizens to recognize the representatives that bear the banner of their interests. It will support citizens across the nation to be better informed, allowing greater respect for the goals of representation that are uncommon to any citizen's locality. Our progression is built on optimism rather than pessimism; this intimacy will provide informed choice and endorsements, thereby strengthening our unity. A better understanding between representatives and citizens should be expected along with providing the representatives with better tools to conduct their job.

At this point in the writing of this proposal, a devastating shooting has occurred at Marjory Stoneman Douglas high school in Parkland, Florida. I believe that somehow, in recognition of our posterity, this event has increased concern for an issue that should have been addressed in previous decades. The Second Amendment refers to the right to keep and bear arms but does not define "arms." From the time that the Constitution was written to today, an armament as an extension of one's person could be defined in many ways, as a grenade launcher or a pellet gun or many other descriptions. Further, the Second Amendment makes no mention to define with any specificity, the emissions of the arms. Should they be defined to only shoot lead, or marshmallows, or miniature exploding bombs? It is the rights given us in the Second Amendment that are left open to debate and definition. Regardless, we the people have ordained our Constitution, to ensure domestic tranquility, among other purposes. In the hierarchal sense, the Second Amendment serves as an insurance policy and is an instrument that serves the purpose of the Constitution, to which we have ordained. At Stoneman Douglas and other identifiable instances, the blessings of liberty to ourselves and our posterity, have not been violated by gun violence in social settings, however. It is our insurance of domestic tranquility that is being violated. This is the debate. The articles and amendments of our Constitution are utilized to fulfill the purposes outlined in the Constitution as ordained. The purposes outlined and ordained in our Constitution's Preamble are not open to debate and have never been debated. As a people we see the purpose and ordination of our Constitution as flawless, and yet some of us see amendments, which are used to fulfill the purpose of our Constitution as ordained, to be flawed.

The relevance of this debate, over guns and gun violence, to the concept of this proposal is important because it will inevitably drive different arguments to create CVIs with the purpose of influencing representatives to make informed decisions respecting the people's wishes. For sure, a member of the NRA will create a CVI. For sure, members of other organizations and individuals seeking to curb gun violence will create CVIs. For sure, every approach and opinion towards this debate will create CVIs. For sure, the influence previously placed upon representatives, by virtue of the organizations that have propped them into the position of their success, will be mitigated by the citizens. For sure, the citizens themselves, through the dedications to the CVIs that represent their opinions, will work out the issues of the debate and promote a resolution. Finally, the citizens will become an effective part of the establishment and they will not be overshadowed.

Naturally, this proposal allows for one concern to lead onto the next, and again, lead onto the next, and so forth. Some citizens may believe that their representatives' integrity toward them is being compromised, and those citizens will have the right to create a CVI to address that concern. This proposal creates the checks and balances necessary in our entire governmental establishment by including the citizens.

I am as opinionated as the next person. We all should be able to express our opinions with measurable influence, and this proposal does this. I, equal to every other citizen, will only be able to create one CVI. I will seek to establish a CVI that represents an issue dear to my heart. My concern with information, how it's presented as well as its validity, needs to be addressed. I am sickened by the indulgence of falsification, lies, and misconstruction of information. Aside from my greatest concern, many other issues of political, social, and personal consequence bother me. I will be fortunate to identify a few of those issues and make donations towards CVIs that reflect my opinions.

Every day, my attentiveness to the happenings around me, locally, nationally, and throughout the world, brings me information to which I form opinions. When I absorb information on a daily basis, I relate how this proposal can be effective in providing discussion and resolutions to the issues. Unless I shut myself off to the outside world, I absorb a greater amount of information about issues that we continue to debate and need correcting. Unfortunately, the news of our times rarely brings a smile to my face. I feel a responsibility to be part of the solution for the issues surrounding me. I may not be right about everything, but I will be able to express my opinion and have that opinion carry some degree of weight.

# 3.

## *PROCLAMATION*

# 3.1.

## *Declaration*

I DECLARE, FOR THE PURPOSE of gaining economic equality and influential recognition in the writ of American democracy, these truths to be just cause for a constitutional amendment.

That the integrity to address the citizens' concerns, to promote the general welfare, is inequitably compromised by influence substantiated through monetary donation made legal by government and its elected and appointed representatives.

That influence, inescapable throughout human history and substantiated through monetary means, must be tolerated in a decided and limited degree, to which degree is constitutionally undeclared.

That the concept of equality for all citizens, in order to form a more perfect union, has been acknowledged through the course of time by the government and its elected and appointed representatives.

That the issue of inequality for all citizens, in order to form a more perfect union, cannot be dismissed by the government and its elected and appointed representatives.

That economic equality for all citizens, to secure the

blessings of liberty to ourselves and our posterity, has not been brought justice by the government and its elected and appointed representatives.

That the government and its elected and appointed representatives rely upon the citizens to promote the general welfare, which reliance has neither been identified nor returned in any form of equitable influence, substantiated through material value, representative of each citizen.

# 3.2.

## *Amendment XXVIII*

SECTION 1. THE RIGHT OF the citizens of the United States to possess a "Citizen's Value," applied solely to a "Citizen's Value Initiative(s)" as an instrument of influential representation, shall not be denied or abridged by the United States on any account.

Section 2. The annual applied monetary total of "Citizen's Value" shall not be exceeded by application of all other monetary and material value(s) combined influencing representation and potential representation.

Section 3. Congress shall have power to enforce this article by appropriate legislation.

# 32.

# 4.

## *THE NEGOTIATION*

# 4.1.

## *Proposal of Law*

AS A LAYMAN, I PUT forth this proposal as concept, pioneering a trail for many to follow and widen and repair and make comfortable for those who will follow behind them.

1A: This amendment will establish a "Citizen's Value," whereby such value will be deemed equal for every citizen and for which the value will be determined as a result of two censuses conducted simultaneously every eight years and applied as a "Citizen's Value.." The "Citizen's Value," as determined by the census, will be the result of the total number of living citizens, determined by the average taken from a single year, divided into only and exclusively the gross total income of all citizens combined in that same year. The resultant figure will equally represent each citizen as their "Citizen's Value." Such "Citizens Value" and no more may be used solely and exclusively as donation(s) to any registered "Citizen's Value Initiative." Such initiative, legally registered as a "Citizen's Value Initiative," will collect donated funds drawn solely from all or part of each citizen's designated donation. The annual sum of each citizen's donation(s) will not exceed a 'Citizen's Value" as applied for that given year. Each citizen will annually declare their "Citizen's Value" donations to the IRS Department of Citizen's Value Administration.

1B: A "Citizen's Value Initiative" may be created for the purpose of influencing any concern that is purposefully opinionated as declared in a single registered statement representing the "Citizen's Value Initiative's" purpose; such statement will be made public and will not exceed 50 words. Such influence may be legally used toward any means to advance the concern declared, including direct contact with elected and appointed government officials at all levels of local, state, and federal government. A registered "Citizen's Value Initiative" will not invest with, nor profit from, any sums collected and will maintain a not-for-profit status. Each individual "Citizen's Value Initiative" will make annual declarations and filings to the Internal Revenue Service Department of Citizen's Value Administration, and make public its income, itemized expenses, and balance sheet with any and all expenses to be no less than fair market value.

1C: The Department of Treasury will establish an independent department subsequent to the IRS, the IRS Department of Citizen's Value Administration. The IRS Department of Citizen's Value Administration will annually collect each and all 'Citizens Value Initiative" reports to be combined as a single report. Said report will be mandatorily and annually delivered before the first day of October to the public and all three branches of federal government, legislative, administrative, and judicial. Said report will be reviewed by all three branches of government within 90 days of receipt, to include a summary disclosure made public by each branch of government of said reports' cognoscenti, to include any intentions toward action as resulted from information provided from the report.

Ai: For any given year the United States of America will recognize with title, "Citizen's Value Equitable Allotment," the whole of one percent of the established "Citizen's Value" as one hundred percent tax free and deducted from each citizen and citizen dependent(s) gross income prior to and before any calculation. Any amount up to one percent (1%) inclusive of a Citizen's Value Equitable Allotment will be accountable as payment to taxes owed provided said citizen and citizen dependent(s), upon declaration, donates that amount to a/any 'Citizen's Value Initiative(s)." Congress will recognize the remaining ninety-nine percent (99%) of the established "Citizen's Value" for any given year as taxable and nondeductible.

Bi: The creation of a "Citizen's Value Initiative" is available to any citizen and may be initiated with preregistration with the IRS Department of Citizen's Value Administration. Preregistration of a "Citizen's Value Initiative" will declare a title/name, such title/name independent from any title/name in use and/or preregistered at that time. Preregistration will require all of: the name of the principal, the title/name of the proposed "Citizen's Value Initiative," and a registered "statement of purpose" not to exceed 50 words. Each "Citizen's Value

Initiative" "statement of purpose" will be irrevocable from preregistration to termination. The citizen and creator and registrar will be the same individual and of legal age to vote. Each citizen of age will be limited to one preregistration simultaneously.

Bii: Preregistered "Citizen's Value Initiative" will meet requirements prior to approval and indoctrination. Such requirements will be: the name of the principal; the title/name of the "Citizen's Value Initiative"; the same preregistered "statement of purpose" as registered; a petition declaring the same registered "statement of purpose," an explanation of "Goal(s)" not to exceed 100 words, an explanation of "Intention(s) Toward Achievement" not to exceed 100 words, signature and endorsement by a minimum of 50,000 (fifty thousand) citizens collected in the same year; mandatory and fully nonrefundable "primary donation" of each endorsed signee "Citizen's Value Equitable Allotment" in the year of process, preregistration to approval.

Biii: "Citizen's Value Initiative," upon approval declared by the IRS Department of Citizen's Value Administration, will be legally documented by Congress.

Biv: Congress shall have power to enforce. The citizen and creator and registrar will be the principal of the legally documented and registered "Citizen's Value Initiative." A "Citizen's Value Initiative" is limited to one principal. A citizen is limited to be principal to no more than one "Citizen's Value Initiative" simultaneously. Any citizen candidate or holder of elected or appointed public office, federal, state or local, shall not be principal to a/any

"Citizen's Value Initiative" simultaneously. The IRS Department of Citizen's Value Administration will assign identification and distribute/deposit the "Citizen's Value Equitable Allotment" "primary donation" to a single account in the name of the registered "Citizen's Value Initiative" for the purpose of monetary initiation. Each "Citizen's Value Initiative" will maintain solely one account for the transaction of monetary funds. The single account holding the monetary funds of a "Citizen's Value Initiative" will be located in any state within the United States and will contain the identification code assigned by the IRS Department of Citizen's Value Administration. In the year following legal indoctrination, before the first day of February, the IRS Department of Citizen's Value Administration will collect reimbursement of administration fee(s) prior distributed for the purpose of monetary initiation. Thereafter legally documented, the IRS Department of Citizen's Value Administration will annually collect funds, as directed by Congress, equal among "Citizen's Value Initiatives," for the purpose of administering this amendment.

Bv: A/any deviation by a "Citizen's Value Initiative" from its declared "statement of purpose" judged as an "obvious redirection of citizens donations" will result in the forced termination of a culpable "Citizen's Value Initiative." The termination of a "Citizen's Value Initiative" may occur at any time. Termination of a "Citizen's Value Initiative" will require a statement of disassembly and a full accounting at termination delivered within 30 days to the IRS Department of Citizen's Value

Administration and simultaneously made public. All funds remaining at the time of termination will be collected by the IRS Department of Citizens Value Administration and utilized toward maintenance of this amendment.

Bvi: The IRS Department of Citizen's Value Administration will impose an annual fee equal for each registered "Citizen's Value Initiative." Said fee will be the total cost of administration imposed upon the IRS Department of Citizen's Value Administration divided equally among all registered "Citizen's Value Initiatives" in the prior year. Said fee will be collected before April 30 of each year. Any "Citizen's Value Initiative" incapable of making full payment of the imposed administration fee before April 30 annually will be forcibly terminated with any and all funds remaining seized and applied to the IRS Department of Citizen's Value Administration's cost of operation.

Bvii: Each "Citizen's Value Initiative" will maintain a singular declared place of business. Such place of business can be relocated solely once per year requiring reregistration of the location. Each "Citizen's Value Initiative" may maintain physically located satellite offices. Such satellite offices must be no more than 50 in total and no more than one in each state. Each "Citizen's Value Initiative" will establish its place of business in nonresidential location(s) within 45 days of approved registration. Each "Citizen's Value Initiative" establishment of satellite office(s) will be restricted to nonresidential location(s). Each "Citizens Value Initiative" may invite contact with government representatives, federal, state and local, restricted to locations where said "Citizens Value Initiative" has a physical office common to the boundaries described as the government representative's locations as restricted. A "Citizen's Value Initiative" may extend no more than five invitations to each individual government representative annually.

Bviii: Each "Citizen's Value Initiative" may employ the principal and additional persons. Payment of employment to the principal will be restricted to one and one-half that of additional persons employed at a/any "Citizen's Value Initiative." Payment of employment to each additional person(s), other than the principal, will be restricted to the individual average annual income in the United States during that same year as declared by the Internal Revenue Service.

Ci: Each "Citizen's Value Initiative" will maintain the privilege of direct contact with sitting elected and appointed representatives of the United States government, including the President and the president's Secretaries of in the Cabinet, Congresspersons, and Supreme Court justices. Each "Citizen's Value Initiative" will maintain the privilege of direct contact with sitting elected and appointed representatives of State governments, including the Governor and the governors Secretaries of Cabinet, Congresspersons, and Supreme Court justices. Each "Citizen's Value Initiative" will maintain the privilege of direct contact with sitting elected and appointed representatives of local governments without discount. Such contact initiated by invitation from a "Citizen's Value Initiative" cannot be refused once per year by each representative. Said representative will be present to attend such mandatory contact initiated by invitation from a "Citizen's Value Initiative" that is accepted once per year. Any contact accepted from invitation by a "Citizen's Value Initiative" in excess of mandatory contact may be attended by appointee upon the representative's discretion. Such invitation made after October 1 annually may be appointed to the following year at the government representative's discretion. Government representatives may accept simultaneous invitations and conduct such meetings simultaneously at their discretion. Such meetings with individual or multiple "Citizen's Value Initiative(s)" may only conclude and be dismissed upon mutual agreement of the government representative and the appointed representative of the "Citizen's Value Initiative(s)." Meeting(s) of direct contact may take place with use of communication devices upon the mutual agreement of the government representative and the appointed representative of the "Citizen's Value Initiative."

Cii: Contact will be made in the physical boundaries of the government representative's location restricted specifically to the nation's capital or primarily the state of representation/jurisdiction or secondarily the state of declared residence. The location and time of such contact will be dictated by the government representative within the boundaries previously described and within 90 days of invitation. Response is required to any and all invitations to government representatives by a/any "Citizen's Value Initiative(s)." Response will be declared publicly within

10 days of said invitation's date of record. Such public declaration will include the invitation, a statement of purpose, its refusal or acceptance, and upon acceptance its time and location.

Ciii: Government representatives may meet without invitation and upon their discretion with a/any "Citizen's Value Initiative(s)" and with any frequency. Government representatives will meet with a/any "Citizen's Value Initiative(s)" solely in locations where the "Citizen's Value Initiative(s)" has a physical office common to the boundaries described by the government representatives. Each and every meeting initiated by a government representative with a "Citizen's Value Initiative" will be immediately and publicly disclosed with full content as well as the time and location of such meetings.

It is a felonious crime: for a citizen to donate and/or misrepresent their annual donation declaration other than prescribed in this amendment.

It is a felonious crime: for a "Citizen's Value Initiative" to collect sums from sources other than the one(s) solely described in this amendment.

It is a felonious crime: for the delivery and receipt of any funds derived from a "Citizen's Value Initiative" to be distributed personally other than prescribed in this amendment.

It is an illegal act for a "Citizen's Value Initiative" to expense collected funds toward a/any misrepresentation and/or deviation from its statement of purpose.

Any conviction for an illegal act in the execution of this amendment will result in termination and retribution without a safe haven to include legal fees.

Any conviction for a felonious act will result in minimum three years' incarceration of the principle, full
retribution without safe haven, and a "Citizen's Value
Initiative" termination where applicable.

# 5.

## *IDEALS AND INTENT*

THE COWBOYS GATHER TOGETHER AND compare notes on which cows are the leaders. The next day, when they begin their drive, those cows are positioned to lead and the herd is behind them. It's time to get moving and the cowboys yell "Yeehaw," or shoot their guns, or do whatever it is cowboys do to get the herd moving. When they yell or shoot their guns, they influence the herd. The herd has good leaders, so once the leaders are moving in the right direction, all is well and the drive begins. As long as the cowboys can nudge and influence the leaders to go in the right direction, the drive goes well. Inevitably, some cow in the herd gets tired of looking at some other cow's ass. So the cow says "I've had enough of this, I'm outta here" and turns stage left to exit. The cow wanders off away from the herd for some distance. A cowboy notices and goes to rustle the cow back to the herd. All this time, the cowboys have been influencing the herd to stay together and move in the direction they wish. Now, this cowboy has to get out in front of this runaway cow and get it turned around. If this cowboy is any good, he will keep some distance and block the cow from going any further away from the herd. The cow still wants independence and turns a little this way, and then turns a little that way, intending to go his way away from the herd. As he does so, the cowboy continues to move a little this way, and a little that way, to block him. The cowboy is no longer influencing the cow as he was when it was in the herd. Now, as he repositions in front of the cow, as if to say "You're not going to get past me," he has turned influence into suppression. The cowboy is good at what he does and he suppresses the cow from going in the direction it wants to go. He gets the cow turned around, and then goes back to influencing the cow to join the herd. "Be a good little cow now and do what you're told."

Okay, maybe I watch too many Westerns. I certainly don't know a damn thing about being a cowboy. I imagine if the cow were that determined to leave the herd, he would have to be roped and dragged back. This would amount to another form of suppression, but more brutal. Of course if the cow were a real bad ass and showed no intention at all to return to the herd, the cowboy could just shoot him and have steak for dinner. This, and continued torture verging on death, are perhaps the most brutal forms of suppression.

I have discussed influence and have identified its presence or absence in our lives. It is important to note that a greater possession of influence offers a greater opportunity to assert suppression and, likewise, a lack of influence narrows the availability to assert suppression thus limiting control. Suppression is a tool or tactic used for control. The long endured and distinctive practice of suppression to gain or maintain control over a mass of people through politics and in government has been used as, and thus becomes, a political ideology. With regard to control in governance, suppression begins when influence isn't getting the job done. Suppression becomes identifiable when the power of influence dissipates so significantly it becomes inconsequential, and the need to put down a desire that veers away from the ability of control comes into play. Suppression starts with no, or you're wrong, or stop right there, and continues on toward the incorporation of physical dominance. Suppression doesn't listen once its course is decided upon. After suppression is initiated, it only asserts. The dictionary does not recognize the word "suppressionism," which is amazing when we consider its power: a calculated tactic, a system, or a philosophy of prevention and constraint intending to control. Brutal suppression relies on physical tendencies to put someone or something down. Material suppression relies on the denial of money and goods to put someone or something down. Information suppression relies on communication and mental infiltration to put someone or something down. Initiating influence is the tactic of trying to get someone to do something. Initiating various suppressions are the tactics of trying to stop someone from doing something. Influence and suppression are the tools used to gain or keep power.

A Communist leader may see a threat in an individual gaining public support for reform and will use brutal suppression to put that person down. It is not implausible that the person is jailed and found guilty of some ridiculous charge. Then their guilt is used to influence a decision that sanctions suppression. As a result, that person is no longer eligible as an opponent to the Communist leader. Totalitarian leaders use brutal suppression a little differently. They keep the herd of four-legged cows busy doing a three-legged dance. When one stops or refuses to dance, they are thrown into jail and sometimes the key is thrown away. God bless Nelson Mandela. The leader of a democracy has the option to use tactics of suppression on materials and information to keep the populace at bay. Deny funding to segments of the opposition, the buck stops right here, suppress from them their material needs used to forge social aspirations. Tell them no, you're wrong, belittle them, call them names and issue a threat of suppression every day. Try to have it appear as a positive influence in an attempt to convince them that the leadership has earned their loyalty and support. Good leadership entails using influence that motivates loyalty and sponsorship. Bad leadership, with its absence to instill positive influence, eventually turns to some form of suppression, thereby making a brutal, material, or informational demand of loyalty and sponsorship. However those demands are posed, if the cow finally turns around and heads back to the herd, he ain't happy!

Our Declaration of Independence was written with the concepts of purity and innocence in mind. "All men are created equal." How beautiful, yet how corrupted the debates became when it was time for its practical application. The expanse of time in which people have suffered and fought and bled and died to retrieve the purity and innocence of that declaration displays an historic use of suppression tactics. The claim of immediacy to an ulterior responsibility has been used over and over again, diverting us from pursuing ideals. The acquiescence to those responsibilities has permitted us to deviate from our chosen path and delay the desire to cleanse those ideals. For some, an ideal is abandoned but not forgotten in the wake of a responsibility. They see a purpose to maintain and preserve that ideal for the ambition of its future reemergence and acquisition. Cases of suppression have identified responsibilities, worthy or not as foundational components, causing us to shuffle priorities and to shift our focus away from an ideal. To have declared equality among all men and permit the ongoing use of slavery must have been an anguishing responsibility for all—except, of course, who enjoyed the fruits of suppression. These individuals who wrote the Constitution employed a primary responsibility in abundance, to forge an agreement toward creating a nation. Through the necessity of that responsibility, those who sought to deny freedoms were able to stop idealists from completing a component in the concept of equality. They successfully suppressed equality and freedom for all people by understanding and using to their advantage a primary responsibility: that freedom would be useless without a nation granting the exercise of that freedom. We understand and have accepted, in at least this instance, the play between responsibility and idealism, the confrontation of idealists and those who have used tactics of suppression.

Is the way in which we individually envision our personal and social responsibilities the crux to our idealistic advancements? Is there reason to doubt the idealistic advancements that have been achieved and witnessed in the past 227 years? Should we have doubt in a world that has witnessed slavery, anti-Semitism and a host of other suppressions, a world that has fought in earnest at the expense of all men, forced by the ideal of good over evil, to cleanse us of suppressions? We need to learn by identifying those suppressions and how their contributions have played in the cause of historic inabilities and failures. We will prosper when we can identify and avoid the point at which our individual expression of personal and social responsibilities turn from influence and become a form of suppression. Our desire to maintain the necessity of an ideal and its hierarchy, using responsibilities as building blocks and not suppressions, will allow our values of growth and equality to endure.

Of a republic: I have listened to explanations of how our democracy is not at all a democracy but a republic. I understand this position. The key point seems to be that the Constitution provides nothing more than a set of rules that are attainable. The sense that, love it or leave it, this is the best that can be done, became the most prevalent ideology in support of it. In a practical sense, I gathered that this viewpoint of governing meant fending for yourself and taking full responsibility for where you end up. Anyone who has put any effort whatsoever into the ownership of their existence understands this perspective.

Of a democracy: In general, most Americans describe our governance as a democracy, not a republic. Many people perceive that a democracy is intended to be less individually isolated and more participatory and inclusive. As good a set of rules as those may be, the Constitution elucidates the continued striving to meet goals that have not been met. The most prevalent sense is that the Constitution can do better to meet the ideology that was espoused in the Declaration of Independence and the Constitution's Preamble, "All men are created equal . . ." and "We the people . . ." respectively. In a practical sense, I gather that this viewpoint of governing means to fend for and take full responsibility for one's self and share social responsibilities that provide for the common good. Anyone who is willing to do more and go beyond their personal standing understands that this perspective permits limited opportunities for those who appear to lack effort, to defer their personal responsibilities and take advantage of social offerings.

Of a republic or a democracy, the conceptual desire to implement our personal responsibility is common. Consistently attending to our personal responsibilities has a positive impact on our social setting. We know the majority of all citizens maintain, even at a minimum, a duty to uphold a level of personal responsibility. Regardless of our conservative or liberal tendencies, the recognition of our neighbors' desire to fulfill their personal responsibilities should bring us together. Furthermore, that recognition and any excesses thereof enable self-worth to which wealth resulting from that enabling is not self-contained. Conservatives and liberals, individually and in their own way, give to society. That offering to give, and the recognition of our neighbors to have value equal to ours, is beneficial to society beyond the value and worth of each citizen. The intent of enabling self-worth, acknowledging personal responsibility, incorporating social responsibility and participation, will provide an immeasurable social profit incomparable to the Citizen's Value itself, when so constitutionally granted.

It has been said that the origin of a conceptual or quantifiable substance must be healthy for any of its extensions to prosper. That the extensions should forfeit themselves for the health of the origin was sometimes necessary, and that the origin itself should draw enough to suffice but was meant to give its most for the good of the extensions. Summing up this balancing act and relating it as a necessity toward growing healthfully, I fully believe the meaning of what was professed should be applied from many perspectives, personally, socially, and in the way governance is constructed and used. This revelation has caused me to reflect upon the forfeitures that have been made to gain the ideals espoused in the concepts of our democracy. That these forfeitures have been made to nourish the seeds of equality and freedom, and those seeds have prospered and flowered in a society that continues to blossom. The seeds in our democracy are the ideals that have been espoused, not the laws that have been written to execute the ideals. The laws in our Constitution, as an extension of its ideals, sometimes need to be regenerated to allow for new growth. We needn't be worried to regenerate and execute new laws to complete the ideal of equality. The solidity derived from our freedoms will continue to nourish our desire to explore and live our ideals. Our reluctance to revise any part of the Constitution and preserve its simplicity and purity is honorable. However, when the opportunity to grow an obvious extension is realized for its ideal, purity, and simplicity, we must, for the good of our democracy, explore its validity. I am presenting an opportunity to visualize the construction of the laws and a way to execute them that would complete an ideal primary to our political origin. This is the season to fertilize the ideal of equality and permit new growth in our Constitution. Upon our own prospect, we are in a position to implant a new extension of economic equality and witness it in bloom.

Bringing influential equality to the Constitution and the peoples of the United States is not a political debate. The concept is pure and innocent. The practical application can be moderately debated. Instead of using raw figures, such as 50,000 endorsements to create a Citizen's Value Initiative, I would prefer a percentage be applied. It is the writing of the laws in this proposal that can be moderately debated, not the origin. If debate of the practical application bleeds into and corrupts the concept of influential equality, then suppression tactics will have come into play.

The intent of any constitutional privilege should always be the foundation when legal decisions are debated and rendered, post the creation of that constitutional privilege. As a living and breathing doctrine exercising the function of government in the interest and protection of the people, I tend to believe that such doctrine should reflect the times in which it is lived and not necessarily the time that it was created. It is the concept and intent at the time of creation that should be honored while the application will continue to be redefined through the course of time. As is already the case, legal interpretations of our Constitution continue to be redefined because of unpredictability and anomalies that present themselves as time moves on. It will be to honor this idea, that the intent and concept of a Citizen's Value—that equitable influence shall be stalwart toward establishing greater purity in the concept of democracy—that this amendment be created. Decisions resulting from the inevitability of unpredictable questions should place an equitable citizen's right to influence the governmental decision process first and foremost. It is impossible to predefine the language that would answer every question going forward; therefore the amendment's language should encapsulate the intent and permit necessary flexibility in order to render decisions reflective to the times they are lived.

The preamble of our Constitution sets forth the ideals and goals to which the articles and amendments of the Constitution try to reach. As a layman, I will illustrate a certain absurdity I have deciphered from a statement I have read, taken from Cornell Law School referencing the Constitution's Preamble. "Courts will not interpret the Preamble to confer any rights or powers not granted specifically in the Constitution." I take this to mean the courts will not allow entry as part of an argument, an ideal set forth in the preamble, if that ideal is not addressed in the articles and amendments. In our Constitution, the citizens of the United States are not individually recognized for a specific material value that can be utilized as an equitable allotment of material influence. No citizen can stand in a court of the United States and include as part of their argument the denial or existence of their right to influence because an amendment has never been written to recognize their value or right to influence. Catch-22. It's a funny thing that influential interests have been entertained in court and have been able to argue and fight for their rights.

To continue, I will provide a comparison to illustrate what I believe is contrary to reason and common sense, an illustration of absurdity. Through the existence of the Second Amendment, a contestation in court can argue the merits of an ideal espoused in the Constitution's Preamble. The ideals of insuring domestic tranquility; providing for the common defense; securing the blessings of liberty to ourselves and our posterity, can be used in argument. Gun restriction advocates can legitimately enter an ideal into their argument, by interpreting the ideal's purpose, which is to reinforce the necessity of restrictions on automatic weapons. Their argument is permitted to include the preamble's ideal, to ensure domestic tranquili-ty, which must be entertained because the Second Amendment exists, and they can argue in favor of restrictions due to the continued erosion of this ideal. The paradox is that individuals who advocate for the restrictions of material influence are not permitted to include such arguments that pertain to any ideals of the preamble, such as the desire to establish justice. The ideals of the preamble cannot be included because the Constitution has not granted quantifiable influence, per se, to anyone or anything. If the Constitution hasn't granted quantifiable influence, then influence permitted by special interests has been inserted by lawmakers at their whim. In theory, there should be no constitutional reinforcement to the influence peddled by special interests. Apart from their play of words and enactment into law, lawmakers have never been granted a constitutional privilege to infuse quantifiable influence into government. Quantifiable or material influence used today is inequitable to the citizen and requires restriction, which is not arguable. The citizen is not permitted to argue the ideal of establishing justice to the issue of influential inequality because no such justice of equitable influence is granted in the content of articles and amendments. There is no justice in the peddling of influence!

We must keep our eye on the ball, that is, on the concepts for which we live and die. When one offers their being to protect and serve their country, the concept of patriotism is honored. When one offers their service to help society, the concept of welfare is honored. These concepts bring us together, to live peaceably. Suppression of these concepts divides us, to live in angst. The discussion we ensure relative to this proposal will not be the ideal and intent; it will be the legal extensions to its practical execution, all of which can be attained.

# 6.

## *MOST OF WHAT WE IMAGINE IS WITHIN OUR GRASP*

THROUGH THE COURSE OF DEVELOPING this proposal I had been permitted the opportunity to reveal some of what I was thinking with people who had initiated a conversation involving the politics of the day. Of those many conversations, only one person had admitted feasibility of this proposal. As you can imagine, laying this proposal out in a conversation could be confusing and time absorbing. To understand it requires a great deal of explanation. It wasn't something that could be explained in five minutes, and I found that listening skills are relatively poor, even among educated people. As well, my explanations had never been organized and were lengthy. Asking questions relative to the experiences of those in conversation drove answers that fit explanations I was trying to convey. In large part, many people listened to the point where they envisioned obstacles they believed were insurmountable. In those conversations and when such points were reached, there was no longer interest or time available to figure out the obstacles and how they could be conquered. Those conversations were dismissed not by me but by the people who I perceived to see me as a lunatic, envisioning something so grand that it would be impossible for one person to formulate when it had already slipped by millions of others. My comprehension of tenacity and the belief in one's self has been reshaped through this endeavor.

As a result of these conversations, I have come to understand that most Americans have little to no faith in the integrity of our representation or our government. I would get to points in my explanation to where I would be presented obstacles such as "Why give them the opportunity to take more money?" or "Good luck, they're only in it for themselves" or "No way, they would never let that happen." On a few different occasions I was told, "You're dreaming . . .," and so I am! I've been treated as though I'm insane and yet, as I have hammered this concept through the years, I can see no negativity in what it will bring to the nation's citizens and the ideals of equality. The effect it would impose on our form of government has been questioned to which I see no difference, save that of inclusion. The question of relinquishment to share influence and the consequence of altercation has been raised. To which I say, that minority must acquiesce to the majority, the tables have turned. I have listened and learned more about the perceptions of our government by our citizens, and what I have learned has only strengthened the concept and helped to formulate its practical application.

Every day I wake up with another insight to the truth and reality of this proposal. If I were to continue writing all of which is true about this subject, I will never complete this edition. As it is, I have sketched out with wide strokes the metaphysical concepts and practical applications with sincere simplicity. The intention to avoid tedious explanation and overindulgence is intentional. I have wanted to get to the point rather quickly without creating an excruciating reading experience. Those who require the full depth of this content are welcome to study, question, and converse. They will be instrumental in bringing the concept forward.

I am in the final revisions of my copy and I find myself adding this paragraph. Money is the full context of this proposal. Money is material and correlates a value. Its value goes further than material goods and services. Money and all its material counterparts bleed into influence. Money—its distributions and taxations—are subject to constitutional amendments. Applications of money are included in the Constitution and are subject to constitutional law. In court, that which is entered into matter of discussion from the defense is permitted to be arguable by both sides, subject to the judge's lenience and interpretation of its relevance to the proceeding. Let those defending their use of money to influence government enter their argument into the court of discussion. In court, if either party can find a way to use this as a benefit to their argument, barring prejudice of the judge, it is not objectionable and deserves to be heard. Yes, obligated to be heard because money, value, and the material abstract of its applications are obligated to be heard by virtue of its written presence in our Constitution. Every day I can describe another important and positive relevance of this proposal. Be it so grounded as a business deal between government and the citizens, or a theological admiration of value to all that exists, or its relevance to the realistic necessity and decency of coexistence. An obligation to make this proposal real goes beyond our representation. It is an obligation for each and every person to bear.

I have been told that I am an idealist, which I believe is absolutely correct. I have been told that I have my head in the clouds. Fine by me because only an idealist can see and imagine the way an ideal can be put to use. I understand that what I propose will be a fight. I am not the first idealist and I will not be the last. Hopefully, my ideals will be a thorn in someone's side.

www.ingramcontent.com/pod-product-compliance
Lightning Source LLC
Chambersburg PA
CBHW051025030426
42336CB00015B/2728